Memoirs of a French Courtesan

Volume 1: Rebellion

Memoirs of a French Courtesan

Volume 1: Rebellion

Céleste Mogador

Translated by Kristen Hall-Geisler

Practical Fox, LLC
Portland, Oregon

Translation by Kristen Hall-Geisler
Original title: *Memoires de Celeste Mogador*
Translation copyright ©2024 by Practical Fox

Paperback ISBN: 978-1-7320603-7-1
Ebook ISBN: 978-1-7320603-9-5
Mogador, Celeste
Memoirs of a French Courtesan
Volume 1: Rebellion

Neither artificial intelligence nor large language models were used to
translate, edit, or design this work.

Practical Fox, LLC
Portland, Oregon
www.practicalfox.com

PREFACE

WHEN I WROTE THESE MEMOIRS in 1852, I was ignorant of the future awaiting me; who could have known? It was not my stubborn brazenness that caused me to I write these memoirs; it was not for provocation or moral outrage, as some of those who were quick to take offense said. Before you condemn the guilty, at least listen through to the end of the story. This confession was meant as a defense, a cry from the soul over many volumes. Over the years, I have been the victim of trials I would call unjust, ever since the tribunals brought me before the court in Paris, Chàteroux, and Bourges. My enemies only had one weapon to use against me—the insult—and they served it up with cruelty. They criticized my past to close me off from polite society.

To understand how the love of a petty squabble could mislead serious men, you must follow along with this legal process. I should have asked for support from the judge. He stepped in when certain violations of the laws came up only because they concerned a woman against whom everything is permitted. There, I said it— with a fury that looks like hate. How could my enemies have thought that justice, that mother of us all, would stop at me? What exactly is my crime?

Even in my shame, I saved up a tiny bit of bread for my future. But I was denied even that. All my efforts to that point had one goal: to forget and maybe to erase even a tiny bit of the past. But without considering that the revelations would crush me, my accusers said in font of the whole courtroom, "Here is the story of this woman's life." They were called to order because men of courage don't need a cannon to kill a fly. But they all knew I wanted to testify to the high cost of what I'd been through. These arguments were publicized so that I would seem insane. God as my witness, I did not seek this out.

The statements made against me that everyone else found so distasteful were downright shocking to me. In order to refute these false accusations, I wrote thousands of lines to say one word. But I didn't say anything about the happiness I held onto in my heart, even in a past full of sadness, of regrets, of misery and shame. I wanted to push back against that odious slander for the sake of the person who stood by my side—and who they shredded to pieces. They riveted his name to mine. Sadly, he was exiled, though I defended him with everything I had. I wanted to prove that the little I possessed was mine, since I had paid for it with the death of my morals. I wasn't trying to rehabilitate myself; you can never rehabilitate one who's fallen so low.

But, I repeat, I did not attack anyone—I merely defended myself. I didn't want to inspire any other poor creatures to follow my example, to walk in my footsteps. I wanted to show them the hazards of this sort of life, to prove that an honest girl living in respectable poverty is happier than these degenerate women for whom only a future of scorn and abandonment remains. It was under that pressure that I wrote these memoirs, which have been given too much attention.

If the man who was by my side can be recognized by anyone in these memoirs, I am sorry. But I believed that memoirs should be true and that no one had the right to create out of thin air a single page from the book of their life. Thinking I'd been deceived by my publisher, I wanted to take the pages back, to undo them. I asked to cancel my publishing contract, and at first I won. But on March 7, 1858, the imperial court directed me to fulfill the conditions of the contract.

What was I to do? Make untrue changes in my memoirs because I did not want to hide behind a shadow, to lie to others while trying to deceive myself? What is done is done. I can't change the past; isn't it already too much to have to answer to the future?

So I believe I have proved here that my good intentions were not fictional. I undertook a long and exhausting project because I was frightened by the idea of no longer being loved by the man who, in giving in to his generous impulses, gave me his whole life. I sought to raise my head a little. I believed that acting with great courage could result in some forgiveness. If I have fooled myself, it's an unforgiveable sin, and God grant that I alone should suffer for it.

CÉLESTE

1.

MY FAMILY—A JOURNEY ON FOOT

I DON'T KNOW IF YOU have ever come across this sort of scribbling, which just between us, I will call—only because you wanted it—my memoirs. You asked me for my story. All that I didn't dare say aloud, I am going to write. I am obliged to maintain a little distance and leave unsaid names too well known to be mentioned. But with each step I take, I will try to portray these characters accurately, and I hope that you will recognize them.

I don't want to make a novel out of my life; I'm not trying to clear my name or pose as a heroine. In talking about what I suffered, of what I did—for better or worse—I will tell you everything without reservation, and you will see that it required great courage for me to face the past.

5

I was six when I lost my father. He was a brave and honest man who, before he died, would have strangled me if he had had any idea that, years later, I would be called Mogador.

We lived in Paris, rue du Puits, near the Temple. My mother was busy with her work, which was going well. For myself, as long as my hair was nicely curled and my mother put me in a pretty dress, the rest hardly mattered.

I was ten before I could read, and that was only because I had to for my first communion and catechism. It was impossible to make me learn. As soon as anyone wanted to send me to class, there were endless tears and sobs. It always ended with me getting my way. I don't blame my mother, but I do regret that she let me get away with it.

I was always playing outside in the street. That's where I got the stubborn, independent character that you see in me. I could not stand the games of little girls, and if I played, it was often boys' games. I preferred toy soldiers to a doll a million times over. My tastes were not much like those of my peers.

My family were hatters. There were always five or six workers coming and going from the atelier. These workers, who watched me grow up, transferred all the affection that they had had for my father to me. I was indulgently spoiled.

At this memory of the people who loved me, another quickly replaces it—one that has weighed heavily on me all my life. There was a large man who often came to the boutique. I hated him. I liked to say terrible things to him as often as I could. Since I had been poorly raised, I was rude. But instead of becoming angry, he brought me a thousand little presents and went into raptures over my beauty. He praised my mind and said that if he had a daughter like me, he would be the happiest of men. All his flattery was a complete waste. You have to tell children and dogs sincerely that you love them—or at least make a convincing show of it.

Monsieur G... was a man of thirty-five, very tall. He was, I think, five foot seven, with broad shoulders, black hair, large deep-set eyes, and very thick eyebrows that seemed even blacker than his hair. He had pale skin, a slender nose, and such thin lips that you could only see their pink flesh when he spoke. His black sideburns blended into his silk cravat. I never saw the collar of his shirt, and most of the time he kept his frock coat buttoned, so I always said that he looked like a spy. That was what I called him. He was from Lorraine, and when he spoke, it was astonishing to hear the voice of a woman come out of this huge, sturdy body. He never looked you in the face. I was afraid of him. When he wanted to play with me, or give me something, or take my hand, or hug me, I made a run for it. I would only return after being assured he had left.

Almost a year went by like this. I did not like M. G..., but I got used to him. When I was scolded, he defended me. When I wanted something, I asked for it in front of him. If I was told no, he brought it for me the next day.

I knew that M. G... had already asked Maman to marry him. I also knew that, without saying yes or no, Maman had answered, "I'll see. If I were to give my daughter a stepfather, I would have to be sure that he would make her happy." After that, everything went my way. My childish instincts were spot-on. By flattering me, M. G… was acting in his own interest.

He was a mechanical engineer and a very skilled worker. He had a house in the country, and everyone spoke well of him. The marriage took place two months later.

My mother had only been married six days when twenty people came to ask for money. G… was riddled with debt.

All these brazen people said to her, "You married a criminal. He doesn't have the money to pay us back. We would have told you, but he threatened us, saying that if we kept him from marrying, he would never pay us." My mother wept.

For a yes, for a no, he pummeled me with punches. Our life was no more than a series of violent scenes.

It only got worse, and after about a year we'd gone through all the money we had. My mother sued her husband for separation. We had plenty of proof of what he had made us endure, but the judge said that all women were unhappy: "Be patient. Your husband promises not to beat you anymore."

Friends got involved and brought the two of them back together. New fights broke out. Friends brought them back together again. He did not want to separate.

My mother was so brave! She worked for hard enough for two, and my grandfather was rich. G… lusted after the inheritance.

He fooled everyone with his sweet voice. He said to the judge, "I've been horrible. I love my wife. I hit her because of my quick temper. I promise to start over." And so they were forced by the judge to reconcile.

We lived like that for a year. I became mute; I didn't even dare say when I was hungry.

One night at midnight, G… came home drunk on wine. He came to my room and removed my blanket, despite my mother saying to him, "You're crazy to wake up this poor child and uncover her. It's freezing." G… entered into a ferocious rage, took my mother by her waist, and threw her down the stairs. My mother's poor head hit a corner, and she was covered in blood. She had the courage to climb back up the stairs and take me in her arms, saying to him, "If you touch one hair on my daughter's head, I will kill you."

We had made it down two flights of stairs before she fell, taking me with her as she collapsed. The cold, the fear, the pain, caused me to black out completely. We would both be dead if a carpenter who lived in the building hadn't opened his door.

His first thought was that we should come into his apartment, but he was a young, single man. Thinking that others might jump to conclusions, he thought that it would be better to put us somewhere safe. He decided that we would wait out the day at the local military post.

೫

When I came to my senses, I was in an armchair and wrapped in a military overcoat. A soldier sat near me, warming my hands in his. They had dressed my mother's wounds, and she was resting.

Here's what had happened.

Our young protector had taken us to the post and asked for the officer in charge. Since I was in my nightgown—practically naked—four men were sent to my stepfather's house to fetch my clothes. The solders found a woman in my mother's bedroom. That's why G… had thrown us out. Both were arrested, and they were put in jail at the post where we had taken refuge.

G… wanted to throw himself on us, but he was well guarded.

"I'll kill them both!" he yelled in a fit of rage.

"Hold on," said the officer, "I'm going to take you to the police station so we do this right."

When morning arrived, my mother, who couldn't walk, was placed on a stretcher, as was I. They carried us both to the police chief who had sent G… to prison. Then he had my mother taken to the hospital.

"Rest easy, madame," he said to Maman. "I'm going to provide paperwork so that you can keep your child with you. Your husband will not be getting out anytime soon. If I might give you some advice, leave Paris as soon as you can. Get as far away as possible with your child. That man could do you real harm."

My mother's convalescence was long. Her wounds filled with pus and became infected. The poor woman feared healing more than pain. As for me, thanks to the cluelessness of youth, I found it quite nice in the hospital. Over that month, I became fat, healthy, and refreshed. Everyone adored me. This made me pretty, and it's why I say that I had an incredible spark for my age. I was already happily inhaling praise.

My mother began to get better, and we were assured she would make a full recovery. As our departure neared, the good gray sisters took turns squeezing me in their arms. They covered me with kisses and sweetness. The hospital was so good for me. I was a perpetual enchantment for the long-timers. That's what they called the sick people in the hospital who, while waiting many long years with incurable maladies, witnessed the constant flow of people who came in with the flu. These poor people had seen others come and go: they had seen the living arrive, they had seen the dead being carried away. I remember them still, in the sweetest and most straightforward way—through the eyes of childhood.

In the evening, inside the large chapel of Saint Mary, the sisters made me recite aloud my prayers. They listened contemplatively to this child's voice as it prayed for all those who suffer.

These are chaste and sweet impressions of my first years. The life that I led to that point has little resemblance to what came later. But how many times, amidst the excitement of pleasure and living, I regretted the very things I'm about to make you feel!

∾

The moment of our departure had come. We heard from the police bureau that my dear stepfather was going to get out of prison. My mother would rather die than deal with his return. She was advised to leave Paris.

A woman who worked in the hat shop said to her, "Listen, I'm about to leave for Lyon, where I work for M. Pomerais, who's also a hatter. Would you like to go in my place?"

I thought my mother might suffocate the woman with her embrace.

"Henriette, you've saved our lives. I will always remember that you've done me this favor, and I will pray to God that he gives me an occasion to show you my gratitude."

Two days later, Maman obtained a passport under an assumed name at the price for a vagabond—three sous per league—and we left the next day. Henriette rode with us, along with a cabinetmaker named Honoré who had once wanted to marry my mother. He became my godfather instead, and he was never anything but a devoted friend.

We soon arrived at the station where we were to disembark from Honoré's carriage. My mother parted from her friend Henriette regretfully. Uncertain about the next day and anxious about the distance that we were about to travel on foot, she looked back. But the memory of her friend didn't allow her to hesitate: the fear of anything getting in the way of our flight guided her forward. I burned with a drive to leave. I pulled Maman by her skirts. You could say that the road before us called to me. At that age, sadness is intertwined with happiness when you're looking for it away from home. Henriette cried hot tears and Honoré held me to his heart, but my need to travel was stronger than the emotions of saying goodbye. I tried to free myself.

At this time, the roads outside Paris were still paved and lined with grand trees. As I heard the noise of the carriages and the wind causing the branches to creak and the leaves to rustle, I felt myself vibrating with impatience and happiness. With everything I saw—and moreover, everything I was waiting to see—I imagined an entire world. I said repeatedly, "Let's go."

Henriette gave me a little dress, Honoré a hat of

open-weave straw. Neither of them were rich; nevertheless, they each offered us a little silver.

My mother reassured them, saying, "I have what I need for myself and Céleste."

Their good hearts felt for us, because they knew that we had left the hospital without a sou, but they didn't dare insist. We exchanged sad kisses that were nothing like the sweet ones of worldly people. We pulled ourselves apart and went in opposite directions along the road.

We walked a quarter of an hour in silence. My mother stopped and looked back. I wanted to see what she saw, so I climbed up on the stone that marked a quarter mile. I heard Maman sniffle, and I saw her eyes fill with tears. She said to herself, "No more!"

We walked all day without eating. At eight o'clock, we reached a rest stop and went into a farmhouse that sat alongside the road. We asked for so little that they received us coldly. I was very tired, but misfortune sharpens one's wits. I knew better than to show this man my exhaustion, so I pretended to be happy. I leaped about, and I flirted with people in the house. My manners worked like a charm, and we were treated as if we were rich.

The next day, my mother went to receive her traveling papers at city hall, and our voyage continued without incident to Chàlons. My mother was pious, and thanks to her devotion during my childhood, she instilled in me habits and patterns that cannot be erased. Each time we came upon a church, a cross, a crucifix, we said a prayer and asked God to protect us on this long road. It was endlessly tiring for a woman and a girl who were reduced to walking.

As soon as we arrived in Chàlons, large drops of water began to fall. All signs pointed toward the approach of a frightening storm. We ran, despite our fatigue, to the steamboat dock.

It was stiflingly hot out. I had been so burned by the sun that my neck was covered with blisters, and I was in horrible pain. My mother had paid in advance to secure her seat. That boat left at five a.m., so the girl at the inn where we stayed woke us at four. We went down to the dining room for coffee to find everyone in an uproar.

It was a horrible scene. The Saône's tides rolled in and out with the sea. We could see that the river was high, which made it more difficult to embark. A single plank had been set in place to get the passengers from the shore to the boat. The wind was so wicked that it seemed like it might carry off the plank.

The fear of losing her place on board caused my mother to be reckless. She took me in her arms and tried to get across at a run, but her weight shifted the plank. My mother stumbled and opened her arms, and I fell into the Saône. I was pulled out, in daze from my fall and involuntary bath, but there was no harm done other than my being scared.

Of course, we were in second class. It was a small, square room with benches all around. When I was changed and dry, I watched the people around us. There was a priest with a kind and Godly demeanor. His hair was white, his forehead high, his eyes black, though he seemed young. It was as if his white hair created a halo of respect despite his youthful appearance. There were also two formally dressed workers, a bold woman in a gaudy dress topped with a weird hat, plus Maman and me. We were six all together.

Having reset my emotions a bit, I approached the priest, and I made a point to look in the book that he was holding. Catholic priests, who have no family at all, are kind to children, because nature always knows how to maintain her rules. He signaled for me to approach, showed me the pictures of the saints, and prayed to God with me that He might end the storm. I sat on my knees in front of him, loudly repeating the words that he said quietly.

My energy was drained. Soon enough, fatigue overcame all other feelings. I laid down on the bench in our room. With my head on my mother's knees, I no longer held off sleep.

The sound of thunder woke me with a start. Everyone cried out in despair. The steamboat had been damaged while passing under the arch of a bridge. The smokestack had broken off. The Saône was roiling, its waves furious, swollen, incessant, seeming to have the strength to flood entire towns. They lashed at the steamboat, and we navigated like a vessel without pilot or rudder.

The tempest quieted down as abruptly as it had come on. The curate, who had become my friend, had protected and reassured me while I was worried. As he disembarked, he said, "I told you, my little angel, that heaven would answer your prayer and that we would arrive in Lyon safe and sound."

Good curate, my companion for the steamboat trip along the Saône, if these pages ever fall into your hands, I fear that you will be a bit scandalized by the faults and follies of the one you called your little angel.

2.

MY STEPFATHER

As soon as we arrived in Lyon, my mother had to find lodgings for us. We asked for a room at Célestins, where the shop owner that Henriette had sent my mother to lived. We intended to lodge ourselves nearby, and we found a modest little room in a neighboring building. The woman who rented this room to us seemed surly and malicious.

I've already told you, I think, that my mother had taken a passport in the name of her friend Henriette. The passport, therefore, was for an unmarried woman. When people heard me call her Maman, they looked askance at her.

Our landlord was a woman of about fifty, thin and short. She didn't look all that nasty, but she had a voice so sharp and a tone so dry that it almost scared me. I never passed by her door without walking on tiptoe.

We had two free days in Lyon. Then Maman went to her employer's place and was well received, but she didn't dare tell him that she had a daughter. I was therefore to stay indoors while she worked. The prospect of being alone all day long was ghastly to me. I even became nostalgic for my stepfather and the blows he gave me. If our landlady had been slightly more gracious, I would have spent time with her, but she was as cheerful as a prison door. She didn't like anyone but her fat gray cat.

My mother saw my anguish, so to console me, she made me a thousand promises for Sunday. This only made me cry even harder. My mother began to cry herself. This was her secret weapon against me, and I calmed down. I promised to be well-behaved and hem our handkerchiefs. It must have been a very emotional moment for me to make this promise, because I had a horror of needlework.

We arrived in Lyon on Friday, but my mother didn't begin her job until Monday, so we went for a walk to Brotteaux. We brought along our lunch, and we sat in the shade of a chestnut tree. We were about to eat when I felt something cold and wet near my neck. I was so afraid that I didn't dare turn around. I looked at Maman, who began to laugh so hard that I decided to turn my head. I saw a huge brown-and-white water spaniel. At least, that was what we thought it was, because it was so matted that it was impossible to distinguish any features except its clear gray eyes, its black nose, its white teeth, and its pink tongue. That was my poor ghost. It had approached us just as I was about to put a tart in my mouth. I gave the dog my bread, and in four or five chomps, he had eaten more than my mother and me put together.

When we'd finished our meal, we all returned along

the road. After about an hour, the dog and I were so happy together that he didn't want to leave me, and I found him delightful. We went back to our house, and he followed me to the door. I wanted so badly to ask Maman for permission to keep him, but a big dog eats too much, and we had just enough for ourselves.

The moment had arrived: Maman had her hand on the doorknob. I gathered my courage in both hands.

"My dear mother, we're about to go inside, but this poor dog is too far from home to find his way back. If you would allow it, I'll keep him just until Sunday. I won't be a bother, and we can take him back where we found him."

"You're crazy, my girl. You want to send us all the way back to Paris? Don't you remember that the landlady hesitated to rent to me because I had a child? If I add a dog, she's going to throw a fit."

I knew she was right. I couldn't promise to hide my friend; he was the size of a large poodle. The door opened, and my spaniel entered with me. I said, "Shoo, shoo," but he wagged his tail and did not move. I felt fat tears come to my eyes, ready to fall.

Maman took my hand and baptized my dog as a sign of adoption: "Come on, Mouton," she said. "You'll keep Céleste company."

We were shut inside our room for three days, which we spent grooming Mouton. When he was washed and brushed, I saw with a burst of joy that he was far from ugly. I was no longer afraid to be alone.

Sometimes when my mother was working, she heard people around the shop say that she had very good taste, and her employers began to treat her very well. She told them of her circumstances and my existence. They reproached her for not having brought me along with her to the shop. The woman who ran the shop wanted to come find me right then.

"Don't go," Maman said. "She has a dog that she doesn't want to leave. It's an obsession like you can't imagine."

The woman was determined to come find me despite the dog and to bring both of us along to the shop. I made quite an entrance in the company of Mouton.

I was so besotted with this dog I couldn't talk about anything else. When someone said to me, "You're sweet," I answered, "Mouton is well-behaved." "And are you well-behaved?" they asked me. I answered, "He's not at all greedy."

❧

Many months went by this way. We were quite happy. We received letters from Henriette, who told us everything that happened in Paris. My stepfather had moved heaven and earth to find out where we were. He had come crying to all of our friends, but they knew him well. No one was convinced by his performance. He ran around, drank, gambled. After about six months, he was crippled by debt. It wasn't long before he'd committed some kind of crime that landed him in prison. He hadn't come across anyone malicious enough to reveal our escape to him and set him on our trail.

My mother worked the counter at the hat shop. One day, a man came in and recognized her as she waited on him.

"If I'm not mistaken," he said, "you are Madame G…. I saw your husband two months ago. He's a real vicious man. He said to anyone who would listen that you had run off with a lover. But don't worry, my wife happily put him in his place."

"Be careful," answered my mother, "not to say that you've met me here."

The man made many sincere promises to be discreet.

The first thing that he did when he got home was write to his wife: "Guess who I met in Lyon—at a hat shop, no less—that poor woman Mme G… with her daughter."

It didn't take long before my stepfather knew where we were. Since he didn't have a sou, he had to hire on as a fire stoker on a steamboat with service to Lyon. I've told you that he was a mechanical engineer.

Since we were ignorant of the presence of G… in Lyon, we lived in complete security. Learning the truth was an awful shock.

One day—or maybe one evening, because at four thirty in the winter, it's night—I was walking my dog. I was in the middle of the square when a man took me in his arms and lifted me off the ground as if I were a feather.

I was going to scream, but all of a sudden my heart stopped and my voice caught in my throat. I recognized my stepfather.

He didn't say a word to me. I couldn't get over my shock. It was only when I saw how far we were from my house that I said, "Where are you taking me? My mother is back that way."

"Stay calm. She'll come find us."

I tried to escape from his arms and yell, but he held me so tightly that my bones cracked and my voice died on my lips. He was suffocating me.

"Listen," he said. "Your mother is a bitch. I've been looking for her a long time. She's going to pay today for all the shit she's done to me. I know that she doesn't love me, but you—you're something else. It'll be good when she finds you, but she'll have to look a long time."

I was done for. I took one last look behind us. Each step that took us farther from my mother felt like death.

I was about to close my eyes when I saw my dog following me. All of my courage came back. I was no longer alone. My dog seemed sad; people say they understand.

We went down several streets, then into an arcade. It was the butcher's shop. All these animal carcasses hung in the windows, and there was a gutter that ran down the middle of the alley full of black blood and globs. Smoking torches threw a sallow and somber light over the entrance. It made me tremble in every limb.

We stopped at the entrance to the alleyway. Just as G... put his foot on the first step, I put both my arms around his neck with all the strength I could muster. He wasn't being cautious, the stupid man, because he was counting on my terror. He was about to go down the alley to make me even more scared, but looking to his left, he crossed the road instead.

We found ourselves in a blind alley, and he stopped in the middle. This alley was tall and narrow, and the windows around us were closed. On the ground floor, there was a simple shop with whitewashed windowpanes. This building didn't look like the others, and the street was dark. Going in, my body stiffened, and I called my dog. When G... turned and saw the poor beast at his heels, he kicked him. I felt something so awful in my heart that I gave in to my executioner. I no longer saw anything, I no longer heard anything—except the whimpers of my dog, who was far away and groaning. I don't know if I fainted or if I wanted to see no more, hear no more, and go numb for a bit.

Eventually I heard talking; it was a woman's voice. I opened my eyes and jumped down from the chair where I'd been deposited. I ran to this woman—I pressed so close against her that you would have thought I wanted to become part of her. I saw G…'s eyes dart toward me. I turned my head away and didn't dare say a word.

We were in a strange kind of room. It looked like a café, but it wasn't. There were chairs, tables, a counter, liquor, and many women in revealing dresses. One of these women was next to G…. I had been put down near her. She had a raspy voice and nasty way about her. Two other women were at a table along with two men; in the middle of the table was a blue and red flame that fascinated me and gave a diabolical air to the people around it. Two other women were playing cards.

I saw yet another woman behind me working on a dress for small child. She seemed younger than her companions, and she was dressed more modestly. She left off her work and looked at me. I saw her face clearly. Her eyes were kind, and her face, which was not pretty, had something sweet that drew me to her.

With instinct born of fear, I examined this boutique where I was imprisoned in search of an escape route. The frosted windowpanes didn't allow me to see outside, and the door to the street was blocked off. I jolted in surprise. The nasty woman next to me had been about to drink from a glass of clear yellow liquor, which spilled all over her.

"Fucking imbecile!" she yelled. "Now my dress is stained." She shoved me so hard that I stumbled a few steps. I remained in shocked silence, not daring to raise even my gaze.

A second later, I felt someone tugging me gently by my sleeve. It was the girl who had been doing needle-work. I took her outstretched hand and gripped it with all my might. She sat me on her knees, and my heart relaxed a little.

The two women who were at the table with the men said to the woman was nearest G…, "Hey, Louise, do you want punch?"

"Non," said the one called Louise. "Your treacle is fine for children. I like plain brandy better." She finished off the glass that had been the cause of my disgrace. Then, turning to G…, she picked up their interrupted conver-sation. "You said that this kid belongs to you? You should have left her at your place. The rules are very strict."

G… kept his silence. He slowly emptied his glass. Once he'd worked out what he wanted to say, he began, "I was married eight years ago. I loved my wife, but she deceived me. It's a tragedy. She treated me so badly that I separated from her, but the laws are unfair. They give custody of girls to their mothers. My wife lives here in Lyon with her lover. I came from Paris to take back my child, and I intend to leave tomorrow. But I'm afraid they're going to come looking for me tonight. I figured I wouldn't be discovered here. We need you to take both of us in."

I let out a long sigh. I didn't dare say anything to the woman who held me in her arms, but I looked at her. She understood and squeezed me gently to signal that I was to keep quiet.

La Louise said to G… that she understood what he'd done, but that all the same I didn't seem to adore him.

He would be better off leaving me.

"It's true," said G…, "that the child doesn't like me much, but that will come later. She was told that I'm not her father. She was raised to hate me. She'll like me when she's older, and she'll understand that I saved her from loose living and her mother's bad example."

I twitched, but I couldn't escape the woman who held me. I looked at her, and she again signaled for me to be quiet.

G… went on, "If her mother could have saved her, she would have. But then I would have lost track of them."

"Whatever makes you happy," shot back La Louise, "but I don't want her anywhere near me."

My protector adopted a neutral tone. "I'll take her in if you want. It's late now, so it's almost certain that I'll be alone. I'll take good care of her. I know about children."

La Louise smiled at this. "That works for you?" she said to G….

"Oui, as long as she's not allowed to leave."

"Rest easy. She has a daughter that she raised well enough. Go, little one," La Louise said, turning toward me. "You're going to stay with Marguerite. Your father will come for you tomorrow."

I shrank away from her. I was afraid to be touched or hugged by this creature.

As soon as the door was closed behind La Louise, I said to Marguerite, "Madame, are you going to take me to my maman?"

Just then, a loud noise came from the corner where the four people were sitting around the table. A fight had broken out, and they began exchanging insults.

Marguerite carried me into a neighboring room and

said, "Now speak, but speak softly, because your father is next door. There's only a thin wall separating us."

I told her my story as best I could. I said that I wanted to be taken away from here, that my mother would die from worry. I clasped my hands and begged her to go tell Maman. She laid me in her bed, closed her door extra tight, and went out.

After she'd left, I slept. I was miserable, and I was still afraid, but fatigue and hunger rose above my despair. Like all miserable children, I decided to let myself die of hunger. I would stubbornly refuse all food. My sleep was the darkest of slumbers. I didn't hear Marguerite come back in. She was sleeping near me when I awoke. Everything came back to me, and I asked her for news of my mother.

"I saw her," she said. "She seems like an honest woman. I told her where you are. She's going to come, but she'll say someone on the outside told her to, because this man would beat me if he knew it was me who went to tell her."

We heard loud talking in the room below. I let out a yelp—I recognized my mother's voice. I hurled myself toward the door. Marguerite held me back and knocked on the wall.

"Don't you hear the fuss they're making down there?" she said. "There's a woman asking for a child. It could very well be she's come to see you. Come look after your daughter."

Marguerite had guessed right: there was no immediate answer from the next room. She pushed me into the stairwell, waited for a few seconds to give me a head start, and then yelled loudly enough to be heard by everyone, "While I was talking to you, the little girl booked it." The poor girl had to weigh the success of my escape against her fear of making G… irate.

I wasn't yet at the bottom of the stairs when I head the door open. G… threw himself in my path. But before he could stop me, I was at my mother's side. I gripped her in my arms, I drank her tears.

G… hurled himself at us, but all the women formed a wall to shield us with their bodies. My mother had told them in a few words of her situation. Her side of the story had dissolved G…'s lies. The truth had a power that radiated from her.

In seeing that these women were willing to defend us, G…'s fury grew. "I'm going to kill all of you!" he yelled in exasperation.

"It's good that I went to find a cop, then," said Marguerite, who had come in after us.

This had its intended effect. G… stopped—fists clenched, mouth foaming, but he stopped.

Marguerite, despite her young age, had taken me in and kept her wits about her. Taking advantage of G…'s moment of hesitation, Maman and I left via a door that opened onto the courtyard.

G… thought we'd gone into another room. All the women turned toward him to keep him from going anywhere while they waited for the cop. Seeing that the cop hadn't shown up, he thought he'd have time to get us out of there. He went toward the door where we had exited.

"Are you still looking for that poor woman?" Marguerite said as she showed him that the door opened onto the courtyard and from there onto the street. "You won't find her. She's gone, along with her child. Do you hear me? With her child, not yours. You, you're an asshole! Get out."

All the women stared at him. G… had no choice but to leave.

"I'll find them again," he growled as he went. "They will pay for all they've said and done to me."

It was time for him to make his escape. The fury of these women was at its height. They would have beaten him mercilessly. Their good hearts had saved me from great danger.

3.

My Stepfather, Continued

As my mother and I fled my dear stepfather, we ran until we were out of breath.

We were not yet all the way inside the hat shop when my mother called out, "I have my daughter! Hide us or we'll be done for."

They all hugged me. My dog came running to lick me and knocked me over with the force of his kisses.

M. Pomerais said, "We understand your need to find a secure hideout now. You'll be vulnerable here. I'm going to send you to a friend of mine who does wholesale manufacturing. I'll send word to them, and this very night you will leave with your little one. Until then, go up to my wife's room. Your things will be looked after soon enough."

We were barely in the stairway when G… arrived. The workers watched him pace back and forth in front of the shop. Frustrated at not seeing any sign of us, he came in and asked if anyone could give him the address of a woman who, he had been assured, worked in this shop.

M. Pomerais was on his guard. "How do you know the person you're looking for, monsieur?"

"It's my wife, monsieur, whom I seek. She has kidnapped my daughter after ruining me and shamefully deceiving me. I would leave this bi—*wretch* if I had my child. I can't say what name she's living under in Lyon because she's in hiding—that's what I was told—to frustrate both justice and my search."

Pomerais wanted to take the broom and shoo him out, but he realized that it was in our interest to lie a little, so he responded calmly. "Nothing in what you just told me is a name. I employ fifty workers; as long as they stay in line, I don't ask the details of their private lives. Many of these women have children, husbands, but I don't meddle in their household quarrels. I'm sorry, I cannot give you the information you ask for."

G… became very confused, more so since M. Pomerais seemed inclined to turn his claws on him. "Monsieur, I am so distraught! They've turned you against me. They've fooled you too."

M. Pomerais rocked back on his heels, thinking he might have been too brusque. "You're mistaken; I'm not at all against you. I don't have the honor of knowing anything about you."

"If you knew me, monsieur, you'd know that I'm right and that I am to be pitied. I've told you that my name is G… and that I'm taking my wife back. If she changed her name, that's your sign that she's deceitful. I beg of you, help me find her. As of yesterday, she was here. She's a woman five feet tall, slender; her face is oval, her forehead high, her hair black and shining, her brows black and arched, her eyes a beautiful gray-blue but with a hard look, her nose aquiline and a little large, her mouth large, her lips thin, her teeth straight. She is almost always pale, with very white skin. As for her daughter—I mean, my daughter—she's just like her mother: proud, unbending. She has a wicked little mind that I would reform." Then, realizing that he'd revealed how much he hated me, he added, "She has been so badly raised! That will change. She's smart. Anyway, you know, monsieur, that a child behaves well for her father."

M. Pomerais pressed his lips together to keep from answering G… with the scorn this performance inspired. "I know, monsieur, the person that you have come to describe to me. She's a hardworking woman who seems honest to us. Her daughter—yours—is a charming child. We believed her mother a widow. She told us last night that she was leaving Lyon for a few days without giving any explanation. I don't know where she went, but I would be delighted to hire her on again when she comes back." This said, M. Pomerais saluted G… and turned his back on him.

G… stood stupefied for a minute. Finally understanding that he would get nothing from this man, he left in a fury.

❦

We went downstairs to learn what had happened. My poor mother was dying of fright. Her teeth chattered. She had to make an effort to calm herself.

"It's not for me that I tremble," said my mother. "If I were alone, I would face him. Am I afraid of death?

Me? But my daughter—my daughter!" She squeezed me in her arms, and she dissolved into tears. My little heart beat hard too. I wanted to be huge, huge as the hate that I had for this man.

At ten that night, an apprentice came to tell us that G… had vacated the doorway where he had been loitering all day. It was likely he'd be back the next day.

At half past midnight, we left, accompanied by M. Pomerais, two workers, and the building's concierge. We were well guarded, yet my mother's hand was ice cold. I felt the twitching of her arms as she shook. I told her that all I could give her was courage, and in trying to reassure her, I reassured myself.

Just as we were about to step out, we saw a man turn the corner. When you're afraid of being followed, everything takes the shape of what you fear; thieves take mile markers for policemen. Maman and I clutched one another, and I let out a whimper. Our friends hushed us. A second passed that seemed a century. A gentleman went by without taking note of us. Released from our fear, we looked at him: he was quite short—without any exaggeration, he was two feet shorter than my stepfather.

We went to Guillotière. The way was clear. When we arrived, it was after one in the morning. They must have been waiting for us, because they came to open the door at once. A man of about forty let us in, more short than tall, more fat than thin, with a healthy complexion and good bearing. His curly hair—half gray, half light brown—framed his face, and he was wrapped in a great coat. I could not see him well at first, but he seemed nice to me. His voice reassured me of this.

"You've come late, my dears. I was going to bed."

"Excuse us, my dear Mathieu," said our connection

M. Pomerais, "but this poor woman didn't dare leave any sooner out of fear of being followed. Take her in. There is no reason for her to leave your house at any time. Her beggar of a husband has no money; when he sees that he can't get any at the shop, he'll go away. But he's a hypocrite who needs to be challenged."

"Don't worry," answered M. Mathieu to Pomerais as he set me onto his knee to embrace me. "We will keep close watch, and the little one won't be bored with my boy."

"Come, my beautiful Jeanne, take heart," said M. Pomerais to my mother. "You are staying with decent people who will take good care of you and your daughter. We'll come back for you soon. What a devil! Don't cry. Good night, my dear Céleste. I'll come back to see you."

I kept holding onto the tail of Pomerais's coat because I had something very important to ask him, though I didn't dare. Finally I screwed up my courage and said, "Yes, come see me as soon as possible, and don't forget to bring my dog."

"It's true, without your Mouton you can't sleep, and you'll annoy everyone. But I have to save my own skin, and my wife will be upset if I bring him to you." The door closed behind him.

We walked across the hall. M. Mathieu led us up two floors and said, "Here is your room. It's nothing grand, but even the most beautiful girl in the world can only give what she has."

My mother thanked him effusively. "You are too kind, monsieur. We will be perfectly fine. We only need a little space, but we are going to be in your way. I am ashamed of the predicament I've put you in."

"Bah, predicament. When it comes to doing a favor

for a woman like you, and for a lovely child like your daughter, and for Pomerais, my best friend, it's a pleasure to have you. Leave it for tomorrow. Sleep well; my wife will come wake you. Goodbye, dear!"

He closed the door, and we were alone. I was tired, and I slept.

⁂

When I woke the next morning, my mother was up. She walked quietly so as not to make any noise. She had combed her hair; I had never seen anyone as beautiful. I looked around our room. It was very nice and well-kept. Outside the window, which looked out over the courtyard, there were climbing flowers, and the sun was high above. At last everything seemed delightful. I felt entirely happy.

"The pretty garden, Maman! I would love to take care of it."

My mother came over to kiss me. "You are waking up—good. They're going to come for us. Come on, let's get you dressed." She was so playful with me. She dressed me with such taste, despite the modesty of our clothing, that everyone thought I was pretty.

Just then, there was a gentle knock on the door. We looked at each other without moving.

"Is it all right to come in?" asked a sweet voice.

"Yes," answered my mother.

The door swung open, and woman of thirty poked her head in. "I've disturbed you; you must be very tired," she said, "but I'm going to the atelier early, and my husband said that I should come let you know. Would you like breakfast downstairs or in your room?"

Maman said of course she was ready to follow her downstairs and that she didn't know how to express her gratitude.

"Oh!" said Mme Mathieu. "If I might be blunt, I didn't come looking for you to take you to the atelier. It's more that I gave in to my son's wishes. Yesterday we told him there's a little girl staying with us, and for the last two hours he's been pestering me."

I looked behind Mme Mathieu, hoping to see my new friend. Since he wasn't there, I insisted that Maman finish getting me ready.

We went down to the dining room. There I found a little boy my age, cute as could be. His curly, wild hair was long in the back and cut short in the front. He had the most beautiful eyes in the world, and he seemed as if he might die if he laughed. He leaned his elbow on the table, with his head in his hand. He looked at me as if from the height of grandeur, as if I bothered him very much. But during breakfast he covered me with kisses. By the time we got down from the table, we were such good friends that we vowed to never be apart.

What a charmer! He was the good one, and I was demanding. He fulfilled all my wishes, giving himself entirely over to some unimaginable wickedness just to amuse me. He received nothing in return.

When I got tired of teasing him during our games, I said, "I want to go in there. I'm bored here."

He began to cry, and his tears touched me. I chastised myself, and we were fine for twenty-four hours.

I was so happy that a month went by like a day.

One morning M. Mathieu came into the shop in alarm. He had a letter in his hand, and he held it out to my mother. "Take it, my poor Jeanne. I believe it concerns you. They've called me to the police chief to hear what I had to say regarding M. G...."

My mother looked at the letter and became pale as death. "What have I done to be so unlucky?" she said as tears formed in her eyes. "Will everyone who came to my aid be tormented because of me?" M. Mathieu looked uncomfortable, so my mother said to him, "I don't want to be cause for disagreement in this house. We will leave tonight. According to the court, once a husband, always a husband. He can take his wife anywhere he tells her to go. Leave me to my fate. But what then, good God? Will I be sold off?"

"As if I would let you leave! It is true that I couldn't read the letter from the chief without thinking things were bad, but the leap from that to your leaving is a step too far. First, where would you go? Second, we are upstanding citizens; he could not come to take you from us. You work enough to pay back the advance I gave you. Actually, you work too much; you'll kill yourself. I will go to the chief, and if you have to leave us, we will find another place for you to hide. If you like, I will loan you enough to set up a small household. You will live at your house, we will give you work, and you will pay back our loan little by little. As for Céleste, she is not his daughter, she is yours, and so we will keep her safe. My son loves her so much that he would make himself sick if she left—not to mention, we would love her as if she were our own. Take heart, then; you can't fix this situation with either tears or words. Don't speak of this to anyone. I'm going to go out, and precautions must be taken. I'm going to find a small room for you—one that, if I were to receive bad news, we would be able to take action the very next day."

"You are so generous. I wish I could prove my gratitude, my good Mathieu!" my mother said as she clasped her hands around his.

"It's nothing. Have faith in God, who doesn't abandon honest people. Believe in kind souls, like my wife and me, who will help Providence pull you form this predicament. Above all, don't go outside, and don't let the children into the courtyard."

I heard this whole conversation, and my heart was divided between the two unavoidable alternatives: I would either need to leave the home of my friend Mathieu or be separated from my mother. I went to the study where my friend did his lessons and told him all that I knew.

He stamped his feet and yelled at the top of his lungs, "I don't want you to go. If you leave, and if you take your dog, I'll stop learning to read!" Then he sobbed so hard and so loud that his mother came running. Mme Mathieu ignored the cause of all this dismay, because I too cried fat tears. Then Mouton began to bark, which echoed loudly in the cavernous attic.

"You both can behave better than this! Two big children, eight years old! Well, aren't you two a pair," said Mme Mathieu so seriously that I thought I was a grown-up and became very red. Little Mathieu was not so easily consoled. "Calm down, my dear child," his mother said. "Céleste will come see you if you behave."

He kept crying, and she continued, "She might not even go away. Nothing has been decided yet." And the kind woman held him so tenderly that I approached so that she could hold me too.

After having divided her kisses between us, she tried reasoning with me. "You know very well that your mother is having a difficult time, and you're not making it any easier for her. Take care, my little Céleste. It's an unkind heart that adds to the troubles of Mme Jeanne instead of looking for ways to lessen them." I promised to do better.

M. Mathieu returned at four that afternoon and told us that he had found a room in the home of one of his friends, M. Raoul, a silk weaver who was honesty and goodness itself.

❦

The next day, my mother rose very early. She had been awakened by a bad feeling.

"Take me to your friend's immediately," she said to M. Mathieu. "I'll leave my daughter with you. You'll send her to me as soon as possible, because without her near me, I won't have the strength to do what needs to be done."

She took a shawl and left, reminding me to behave and to not bother the people who wanted to keep me safe. I wanted to latch on to her and not let her leave without me, but I was reminded to obey her. I stifled my dismay.

Mathieu drove her to his friend's. I waited impatiently for his return. When I saw him come in, I ran up to him. He took me in his arms and brought me to the window. He lifted the corner of the curtain and said, "Céleste, is that man out there your stepfather?"

I was so shocked that I couldn't answer at once. I looked without seeing. I clutched at Mathieu. "Where is Maman? Did he see Maman?"

"No, he didn't see her, luckily, but he doesn't need much. She was right to ask me to take her this morning, because I had planned on her leaving this evening. The porter told me when I got back that a man had come around asking a lot of questions. He pointed him out to me. There, that's him in front of the house."

I looked again, and I recognized G…. My mother was somewhere safe; there was no need for us to worry just then. But I spent the evening being restless anyway. I thought I saw G… behind all the furniture, around every corner. I awoke the next morning very tired!

M. Mathieu left at ten in the morning to meet with the police chief. He found G… already in the office and walked past without looking at him.

M. Mathieu said to the chief, "Would you like to move this along, monsieur? I am a businessman; I have sixty employees, men and women, to manage. If each person in my shop lost half an hour, that would be thirty hours lost to me."

"I understand. Here's why I called you in. M. G…, here, accuses you of hiding his wife and daughter. It seems his wife has behaved badly. It's not her that he wants back; he wants his daughter. What do you have to say?"

Mathieu looked G… up and down. Then, turning toward the police chief, he said, "You know me, and we have a good relationship. I give you my word as an honest man that this gentleman is a scoundrel who beats his miserable wife and miserable child. He's lazy and immoral; he only wants to find his wife so he can treat her badly and take what she earns before he leaves her again. Yesterday, when she learned you had written to me, she had no doubt that it was because of him. She saved herself by leaving the girl's birth certificate with me; here it is. You can see he's lied to you. This child is not his. He's only her stepfather. His wife is the hardest-working woman—level-headed, thrifty, trustworthy in every way. Mme Mathieu says that she doesn't know a worker more capable."

"All well and good, monsieur," said the commissioner. He looked at G…. "How do you respond?"

G… was not shaken. "I respond that this man is my wife's lover, that's why he speaks so well of her. If he had the tact to speak to his wife about her, it would destroy your suspicions."

The commissioner frowned and looked sternly at G…. "Be careful. Once accusations are made, they have to be proven." He turned to Mathieu, who shrugged with an air of pity. "You're saying that this woman is no longer at your house, and she took her child with her?"

Mathieu hesitated, but he didn't know how to lie. He answered with a steady voice, "I have the child at my house."

G… pressed his lips together.

The chief said to G…, "You hear, monsieur, that your wife has left. As for the child, she doesn't belong to you. I order you to leave them both in peace."

Mathieu left in triumph, but he read in G…'s face a sinister smirk. So he promised to take extra precautions to keep the location of my mother a secret.

When M. Mathieu went to see Maman that evening, he turned down a thousand streets because he assumed G… would be on the lookout.

My mother could not get used to the idea of being without me. She wanted to come find me. It took all the care Mathieu could summon to settle her down.

"Look, my dear friend, give me three days. In three days, I swear that you will have your daughter. But we cannot be reckless. To that end, I will not come tomorrow. If he follows me when I do return, I'll take a walk. Today I lost him by going through a building that had two exits."

My heart was near to exploding during all their next day's journey. My friend Mathieu went to walk with his father. They saw G… at a liquor store almost directly across from where we lived. Soon enough, G… spied them. He paid his bill and followed them for two hours, until they returned home.

The next day, the same walk. Mathieu and his son went into the building with two exits, stayed in the stairwell a half hour, and left before G… did.

The third day, after dinner, Mathieu said to his wife, "Come on, we need to dress Céleste. I'm sure that her mother is going crazy. If we don't use our advantage soon, she'll do something impulsive."

"I will do well by her," said Mme Mathieu. "God grant that he doesn't come anywhere near you. Our little one is in bed; he should already be asleep. Come along, Céleste."

Taking my hand, she led me to her room. She opened the little room where her son slept and came back with all his things in her arms. I looked at her without understanding.

"Come here so that I can undo your dress. You're going to see your mother."

It dawned on me that I was to be disguised. I got undressed so quickly that I tore everything off. I hadn't seen my mother for two days, and I adored her. The clothes of little Mathieu fit me perfectly. Mathieu's father came to see if I was ready. I leaped toward him.

"Put the little Sunday coat on her; it's not warm out. Pull this down over your eyes. She is handsome this way! Pierre is going to come with us. You will take his hand on one side, little Céleste, and give me the other. There is no danger, but we won't speak just in case. If someone comes up to us, don't make a peep."

Pierre, the butler, came in at that moment. He told us that G… was standing at his post.

"Let's go," said Mathieu, "it's time." He grabbed his jacket, and we three went out. My legs shook. I would have fallen if I wasn't being held up by M. Mathieu and Pierre.

G… followed us. Once he came so close that I thought that he recognized me. But he backed off, and when he saw that we were taking the same route that M. Mathieu and his son had taken before, he left us.

We came to the house where my mother was staying. Being tired and happy to think that I was going to see my mother—or with the residue of fear that I'd had of G…—I could not go up the stairs. I fell to my knees on the first step.

Mathieu took me in his arms. We saw a light at the

top of the stairs, and we heard the voice of my mother.

"Is that you, Mathieu?"

"Oui."

"God be praised! I was about to go out." She was, in fact, completely dressed. "Oh, that's not my daughter! Someone took her from you." She threw herself almost on top of us. "Come," she said. "I will find her."

I ran after her and said in fright, "You don't want to hug me, Maman?"

She recognized my voice, lifted me in her arms, and smothered me with kisses. "Sorry," she said to Mathieu, holding her hand out to him. "I was mistaken. But I have suffered so much believing I'd never see her again. I ask for a little mercy."

The good Mathieu laughed heartily. "It's fine, it's fine, calm down. Our plan succeeded. But I'm more glad that we can do this again if we need to. I will send someone for the child's things. G… is going to give us a hard time tomorrow when he sees that his little girl is no longer at our house. Goodbye! Don't worry, I'll be back as soon as possible, and I will give your address to Pomerais."

I was reunited with Maman and had succeeded yet again in evading the pursuit of G…. But this wouldn't last for long.

4.

THE LYON REBELLION

THE LODGINGS THAT MATHIEU HAD rented for us had a small bedroom and a large room with two windows with views of the docks. The view was amazing. We could see countless numbers of boats going up and down the Rhône. Across the street was a long bridge and, at each end of the port, two structures serving as control towers. All this created such an animated, lively scene that you could sit and watch out the front windows all day long.

The little room could be used as a bedroom, but it was no good for working because it lacked daylight. The only light came from a small courtyard. The wallpaper was nice, the floor tiles a deep red, but our furnishings were meager. There was a little strap bed plus two chairs and a table that had been brought in for my mother.

Mathieu asked Maman to tell him the furniture

45

that she needed, and he kept his word. Two days later, a cart brought us furniture all made of walnut: bed, vanity, chairs, table, mirror. We were going to have a veritable palace. The strap bed was put in the little room, which became my bedroom. The good Mme Mathieu had forgotten nothing—she sent us curtains and napkins. Never had we been so rich. The love of having nice things is such a strong, shared feeling that we passed our happiest days staying home.

When evening came, we passed some time at the home of our neighbor, M. Raoul. When we first entered his place, we were stunned by the rhythmic noise of four workers at the jacquard loom working together and stepping in time. M. and Mme Raoul were excellent people, but so ponderous, so dull, that as soon as we arrived in their drawing room for the evening, I fell into a deep sleep. I missed my friend and victim little Mathieu so much! He would come visit me sometimes. As rare as his visits were, they made me very happy.

We had no sign of my stepfather. There was every reason to believe that he'd taken off again; even so, we always kept our guard up, and we were very careful as we went about town. We spent two months in our new hideaway without anything coming to trouble us.

My mother worked like a horse almost every night. The silk weavers used children to attach the threads to the bobbins. These children, who were usually ten or twelve years old, earned ten sous per day. I watched them work, and I learned how to do it. I was so persistent that M. Raoul noticed and said to my mother, "If you would like, I could take Céleste as an apprentice. She would earn money, which always helps a little. I'll treat her like any of my employees. I won't tire her out."

My mother hesitated, but I begged so much that she consented. She moved her things to work near me.

After two weeks, Maman used my money to buy a pretty little dress for me, and we went to see Mathieu. You're saying to yourself at this point I was being impossibly vain. I thought I was a grown-up because I earned a living. This dress—I bought it. I made such a big deal out of it with my poor little friend we didn't even play that day. Then it was time for Maman and me to go back to our place. Only when I reached the door did I begin to feel sorry for the time I'd wasted. Little Mathieu said not to wear my good dress next time. He told me that he'd rather I wore his clothes again.

Early the next day, I was at work. My mother worked near me and M. Raoul. He raised his glasses and said to her, "You know, my dear friend, that yours is a very sad life—living alone at your age, always working, without holidays or Sundays. Maybe you should try one more time with your husband. Men change; the bad become good."

"Why would you say this to me, M. Raoul?" said my mother in shock.

"Madame, my child, I was that way too. When I was young, I had huge faults, but nevertheless, as you can see, I now am very happy at home."

"If you knew my husband," said my mother, "you would understand that there is no helping him." My mother did not like to speak ill of her husband. She didn't speak of her suffering at all unless she absolutely had to. What she did say was always correct—I am sad, my husband mistreated me, he beat my daughter—but she didn't give details. The kindhearted M. Raoul hadn't seen in these general complaints a serious enough pattern for separation.

"Look," he said, "I don't want to frighten you, but I must tell you what happened yesterday. You had just left when a fine-looking man, well-dressed, asked to speak to me alone. Not knowing what he could want to say, I asked him in.

"'Monsieur,' the man said, 'don't be put off by my name. I've made grievous mistakes, but for all sins there is forgiveness. My name is G…. My wife is staying here, in lodgings that you rent to her. You can see that I am well-informed and that if I wanted to do her harm— as she certainly told you was my intention—I would go straight to her. That could scare her, though, and I don't want that. I came to you, an honest man, to ask you to help me be forgiven. I've been unfair, violent. I'm sorry, and I promise I will not do it again. Tell my wife to try living with me one more time. We would live in this house, where you can judge my behavior. Believe me, monsieur, I am sincere.' And as he spoke, he had tears in his eyes.

"I answered that I had no power over you, but I didn't dare say I didn't know you. He already knew everything. I asked him how he knew your address.

"'The first time,' he told me, 'I sent a messenger with a letter for my wife. After some hesitation, I was given Mathieu's address. I asked about him at the messenger's office, but I saw that I couldn't get anywhere by force. As I didn't have any money, I accepted a job in a nearby town. I asked for and got a good price for building my machines. I came back to Lyon two days later. I sent the wife of one of my friends to M. Mathieu's home. She told them that I had left the city and that she wanted to know Jeanne's address to share the good news. Pierre, the servant, gave your address. I earned eight hundred francs in those six weeks away, and it's all for my wife. You will make her accept it, because I know she's had so much bad luck.'

"I told him that I could not take his money but that I would relay his message."

My mother had listened to Raoul without breathing. "It's all over," she said. "Where can I go that's safe now?"

There was such great despair in her tone that M. Raoul was frightened. "What do you mean, my dear, somewhere that's safe? Don't abandon your life here. What's the harm? He won't kill you in front of me. We're right next door. When anyone so much as speaks loudly at your place, I hear it. With the money he's offering, you could pay off what you owe on your furniture and still keep some in case of emergency."

My mother let out a sob that became a sigh. "You don't see, then," she said, beside herself, "that the thought of seeing this man again makes me insane. If he comes into my room, I will throw myself out the window."

M. Raoul became serious, almost stern, and said, "You'll find a middle ground to settle things! And your daughter, madame, will you throw her, too, out the window?"

My mother slumped her chair and crossed her arms. I ran to her. I couldn't say anything in the face of this immense grief. She was suffocating.

At last her tears came in a flood, and she said, clasping her hands, "My God! My God! You've abandoned me!"

I was more afraid than she was, but I said as I hugged her, "Since he promises that he will no longer do us harm, try, Maman. We're no longer running from danger here."

She sadly shook her head and asked M. Raoul, "What time is he coming?"

Noon bells rang out.

"Any minute."

"I will see him here, in front of you." She got up, left the room for five minutes, and came back with a roll of paper in her hand. "Take it," she said to M. Raoul. "Read this, and you will know the man who pulled you into his web of lies yesterday, and you are about to hear him lie again." She handed him the copy of the request that she had made in Paris to gain the right to separate.

Raoul, after reading it, lowered his head, gave the papers back to my mother, and asked forgiveness for having doubted her courage and her devotion to me.

We were informed that G… was waiting in the next room. Raoul motioned for my mother to accompany him. She followed him, holding on to each piece of furniture as she passed. Reaching the door, she straightened up as if a spring had been released inside her.

G… held his hat in his hand. He turned his back to the window. He moved as if to pick me up, but my mother placed herself between us and said, "What do you want from me?"

"I want to make peace with you," he said, a little thrown off by this question. "I want you to forget the past. I will make you happy; I promise in front of this gentleman. You'll see that I'll make up to you all that you've gone through. Come give me a hug, Céleste!"

It goes without saying that I didn't budge one step. My mother considered. Then, as if she had come to a decision, she bent toward me.

"Go, Céleste," she murmured, "go hug your step-father." She realized that she couldn't do otherwise; G… still controlled her. If she removed her mask of goodwill, he would notice. It was better to go on as if she believed him. Pushing me toward him, she said, "Go ahead, he won't do anything to you."

When I wouldn't move, she said, "See, M. Raoul, my daughter hasn't overcome her fear, if that's what you'd call it. He'd pretend to hug her or give her something, then kick her legs until she had bruises like inkblots. Or he'd pull her braids so hard that when I combed her hair, it fell out into my hands. If she cried and I had the audacity to defend her, he beat me. 'You like her better,' he'd say to me. 'You like your bastard better than me. I'll kill her. I know how to hit like you can't imagine.' You understand, right? This child is scared."

G... had no answer, but his grimace of a smile hid his intention to bite like a snake.

Raoul, moved by my mother's story, looked at him. He seemed to be asking, *Is this possible?*

"You exaggerate, Jeanne," said G..., "but I'll make you forget all of that."

❧

The next day, he moved into our rooms. We felt no consolation at all for this awful situation. He made it seem as if he were happy. He brought his trunks, which weighed on us. M. Raoul gave us the use of an attic space above the hallway outside our door. This attic formed the point of the roof. The house only had two floors above the ground floor, and we were on the second.

G... didn't stay at the house much. He always had money, which he would give to my mother, who hid it to save it for when the right moment came.

Many men came to see him. My mother begged him to meet his friends somewhere else because it disturbed her work, so his outings became more frequent. He no longer came home and rarely slept at the house. My mother concealed her worry, but because the consequences of his behavior could come back on us, she believed she should tell M. Raoul.

"G… does not work. He has money, and he hangs out with shifty-looking men. I believe that he's going to do some evil deed and that he'll implicate us in it. You should have him followed."

Maybe in other circumstances, M. Raoul would have attached less importance to my mother's premonitions, but we were on the brink of a horrible event. The insurrection in Lyon had begun to throw its menacing shadow. M. Raoul, who of course kept abreast of affairs, had already seen the signs that something was going on. He worried as he took in the information brought to him. He learned that G… ran in circles with men suspected by the police and that he went to meetings where they roused men to violence. The police had been fine to us, and I have no pretension, you understand, of judging events I took any part in. But what I can say is that revolutions have a horrible side, and I retained the frightening memories of all that I saw at that time. Business came to a halt; mobs formed in the streets; the workers revolted; hideous men who seemed to have escaped from prison fought the crowds. I shook when I heard death threats and firebombs in our neighborhood.

One day, G… came in with a menacing air, like a man who no longer needed to compose his face. He told us that he had friends coming over, and he ordered us to leave the place to him. My mother answered that she didn't want to leave, that he could go elsewhere.

G… clenched his fists in rage. "I'll be back at noon.

Try not to be here, or I will crush both of you." Then, opening the windows noisily, he added, "Look, Jeanne, everyone is on the docks. A revolution has begun. Three days from now, I could kill you without anyone asking me where you'd gone or how you died. I've done the business of others; now I want to do my own. Your friend Raoul—your lover, no doubt—will be thrown out this window and bled like a pig. The rich are going to dance. Idiots! Who gave us money to serve them! We will no longer serve them, but we will take their money. We will demolish their halls to find their strongboxes." Then, bowing to the ideas of others with the fickleness and cowardice that were the foundations of his character, he said as if to himself, "We're playing for high stakes."

He stood at the mirror to retie his tie. "It would be a shame if a handsome neck like that slipped under the scaffold. But there is no danger; I'm careful. I know how to wait," he said to my mother as he neared her. He looked at her in such a strange way that this statement seemed even more terrible and menacing.

I ran to my mother. He rounded on me, furious. He took me in his arms and squeezed so hard that I thought he would crush me, and then he threw me across the room. I fell, stunned, at the door to the little room where I slept.

My poor mother turned on him like wounded lion. "Coward! Asshole!" she yelled.

But he knew this poor woman so well. He leaned her over the table, took hold of her, and said as he bashed her with his fists, "Shut up, or I'll strangle you!"

Pain and fear kept her quiet.

He drew her close, made her fall slowly to her knees, and went out, saying again, "I want this room at noon."

As soon as the door was closed, my mother dragged herself over to me. I cried quietly. She looked at my arms. Blood seeped under the skin and made a bluish stain.

"That monster! That monster!" she yelled. "Who will rescue me from this killer of a woman and her child?" She took me in her arms and lifted me off the floor. "Let's see. Where are you hurt?"

I showed her my hip and my knee. These had taken the brunt of the fall against the tiles and were all bruised. It was so painful I couldn't hold myself upright. I've already told you that fear made me mute, and I could not speak.

My mother said, "I'm going to put you to bed." I nodded yes. She laid a saltwater compress on me and went down to the pharmacist to look for a remedy.

Time passed. Since she was occupied with me, Maman didn't think to leave our rooms. We heard a muffled noise on the docks.

She looked out the window. "There's a reason for this nightmare—something is about to happen, and chaos will follow. It would be better if he kills me. Death is better than the suffering I endure."

She returned to my bedside. I had a fever, and I asked for a drink. My mother didn't have any sugar, so she went downstairs again. She noticed that G... had gathered a group a few steps from the house.

She came back up in a frenzy. "What should I do?" she said.

I closed my eyes.

"Go to Raoul's! But that would expose Raoul. My daughter—I can't carry you in this state. My God! What am I going do? If he finds...ah!" She ran to the table and picked up a knife. "If he touches my child, I will kill him."

Coming back to me, she said, "No, no! I'm out of my mind. It's me who will be killed. And you, Céleste— what would become of you?" She stopped to listen, then she ran to the door. "It's too late! They're here!"

She grabbed the key, fled into my little room, and closed the door. She leaned over my bed, put her hand over my mouth and her lips against my ear, and implored, "Be quiet, be quiet…"

The door to the main room opened and closed. We heard the footsteps of many men.

"We're not all here," said my stepfather.

"Non," said a voice, "the others are coming. We didn't want to show up together for fear that it would be noticed downstairs. The rich bastard on the first floor would fear for his money. He's watching everyone who leaves the house. I wouldn't be mad if his neck was wrung. I had a massive grudge against him, and then there was the time that he—"

There was a knock on the door; the voice stopped. The new arrivals must have been whispering, because only a muddled noise could be heard. There were probably been eight or ten of them. Little by little, the discussion became more animated, the voices more distinct.

My mother and I could hear with the crystal clarity of fear. It didn't take long before we realized to our horror that in the next room, my stepfather and his loyal acolytes were plotting.

"It's impossible," said G…. "That can't be done without being sure. If things don't heat up while we're over there, we'll all definitely be arrested. It's got to start here first."

Another voice cut him off. "Come on, now, you're afraid of everything. No risk, no reward. By the time things get going here, nothing will be worth anything at all over there. You've got to scare off the chicken to take the eggs."

"Are you sure," said G… in a calmer voice, "that the thing is worth the trouble? That we'll find as much money as you said?"

"Rather more than less," said another voice.

"When's the deal?"

"Tomorrow."

"How much time do we have?" said G…, who still seemed uneasy.

"Six hours at most. It's three miles; we'll leave early in the morning."

The conversation became muddled again. Some of the men left. "Goodbye, until tomorrow evening. Good luck! I'll be damned if he doesn't get a windfall from all that we want to do."

The door closed when the footsteps were far enough away. G… said to the men who remained, "We need to keep an eye on Antoine; he might expose us for nothing. I find him too sensitive. He's not Norman for the glory."

"Come on, now," answered the others. "You two suspect each other. He said yesterday that you're from Lorraine, and that he doesn't tell you everything."

G… stayed silent.

A voice near the window said, "This place is good. You can see well, and you could help."

"At your service," said G….

They all made their way to the window and spoke in low voices, so we could not hear any more. Then the words "Goodbye, until tomorrow" came again to our ears.

My mother stretched herself against me in bed and sighed. "Gone. They've gone!"

I was still afraid that she was wrong. I joined my hands and motioned for her to wait. She did, holding her breath.

After a few minutes, we heard someone walking. They opened the cupboards, closed the windows, and left, taking care to turn the key in the lock.

My mother opened our door and said, "We're locked in. What now?"

She thought for a second, then knocked on the wall we shared with M. Raoul. He came to our door. We called out that we were locked in, and we asked him to hurry and find a key.

"Don't bother," said Mme Raoul, who had followed her husband and come up behind him on the stairs. "Here's the key; it was given to me downstairs. I met M. G… as he was leaving. He asked if his wife was at our place. I told him I had no idea, that I'd been out for two hours. He asked me to give you the key, that he'd brought it along without thinking."

M. and Mme Raoul both came into our room. My mother told them what she'd heard. "He's going to go looting, maybe commit a more serious crime. These terrible men have to be stopped. They're menaces."

"But do you know their names and addresses?"

"Unfortunately, no."

"What do you want to do, then?"

"I haven't a clue, but I'd be a fool to let this happen."

M. Raoul began to calm down. "What could you say? You don't know their secrets. You would put yourself in danger without being useful to anyone. And then, who would we even tell right now, when all the authorities are under threat?"

Maman spent the night close to me. G… did not return.

57

The next day, the sky was black, the day somber. A terrible storm was forming over the town.

Near four o'clock, the sound of pounding footsteps could be heard on the stairs. G... came in, pale, with an evil look in his eye, his clothes in disarray, his tie half undone. Sweat ran down his forehead.

"Hide this," he said to my mother. "I need it." And he threw a sack of money onto the table along with a smashed parcel. Turning back toward the door, he said to two men who had followed him, "Go in with your trunks; it's only my wife. I'll vouch for her."

My mother watched the scene without moving, almost without reacting.

"Let's see," G... said, opening the parcels they'd brought. He pulled out silk dresses, linen dresses, lace, some jewelry. "These frocks aren't worth anything. This can be for my daughter." My mother forced herself back to the present and the dresses.

After having arranged his share of the goods, G... left again without saying a word.

My mother remained quietly thoughtful for some minutes. Then, taking me in her arms, she said, "Let's go to Raoul's. He gave me an idea that might get us away from the odious presence of this man, at least for a little while."

She chatted with Raoul for a very long time. He got up, saying, "Very good. I understand. You can count on me."

The next day, very early in the morning, a man knocked on our door. G… leaped out of bed. Like all those who've done something bad, G… was afraid. He came to hide in my room.

The newcomer asked very loudly, "You are Mme G…?"

"Oui, monsieur."

"Where is your husband? We need to speak with him."

"He is not here, monsieur, but if you leave me your name, I could tell him you came."

"Non," answered the man, "we'll wait downstairs until he returns. He was one of those who looted the… château. Do you have any information on this theft?"

"No," said my mother in a firm voice.

"Be warned, hiding the truth makes you an accomplice. Goodbye, madame." And he went back downstairs.

G… came out of my room discombobulated with fear. If he were in a cooler frame of mind, he would have asked how they had all of a sudden arrived at his hideout. But remorse and fear don't ask sensible questions.

"Jeanne, my good Jeanne, you saved me!" said G…, becoming almost tender.

"For maybe an hour, but the officers will be back to do a search. You only have one option: escaping tonight. Until then, you must remain hidden. There is an attic over the hallway. Put all your things there."

G… didn't make her say it twice.

An hour later, five men came back, making a lot of

noise. G…, hidden in his attic, didn't miss a word of the conversation.

"Has your husband returned?" asked the man who had been there that morning.

"Non," answered Maman.

"I am sorry to say, madame, we cannot take your word for it. We must see for ourselves."

Two of them men came into the main room and my bedroom, and they seemed to search everywhere.

"Nothing," they said as they left, "but he won't escape us. He'll be sold out by one of his accomplices. As for you, madame, we don't want any harm to come to you. We know, thanks to M. Raoul, that you are an upstanding woman and the first victim of this scoundrel."

G… was more dead than alive. My mother did everything in her power to make him leave his attic.

"Let's go, let's go," she said. "All is lost for you if you don't flee far away. Don't waste any time. Take advantage of the fact that they don't think you're here. You have money. Leave."

"I want you to come with me."

My mother looked at him as if to say, *That's too much*.

At midnight, G… left.

Raoul was waiting for us. As soon as he saw us, he said, "Ah, good! You are free of him. He won't dare come back anytime soon; he's such a chicken! He's only brave enough to beat a woman and child. Did my men play their roles well?"

"Wonderfully!" said my mother. "You've done me a huge favor."

The men who had come to scare G… and force him to leave were none other than the silk weavers.

The next day, Lyon was fire and blood. Our building was surrounded. They set fire to either end of the bridge opposite us. That's where the watchtowers were. A lot of flammable material had accumulated there: oils, alcohols, et cetera. The flames escaped from every opening, enveloping an entire vessel in an instant. Then they'd die down a bit.

You could see distraught people throwing their furniture and anything they could save out the windows. You could hear them letting out pitiful cries that were soon lost in the overwhelming roar, which was pierced at intervals by ferocious outbursts of laughter.

When the fire had found new flammable prey, it extended its curtain of flames anew. Everything was gone.

We saw one poor man jump out the window to save himself. He landed badly on his leg, couldn't get up, and was trampled to death by the crowd.

Suddenly a rumor broke out among this gathered mass of men. We could see the group flee in all directions. Troops had arrived at the other end of the docks. The docks became deserted, and it was impossible to make out where those who had taken cover hid themselves. No one opened their door to shelter the rioters, who had laughed when they saw the destruction they'd wrought.

But it was a false alarm. We heard the rhythmic steps of cavalry horses moving away, leaving behind a cloud of dust. The cloud dissipated, and a few tense seconds passed. Nothing had changed. The dark tide of people came together again with even more menace.

The rioters, seeing by the departure of the cavalry that things would be quiet for a few minutes, took advantage of the time they had before new troops arrived. Every door was forced open, every house was invaded.

"Arms! Arms!" they yelled, and they wrenched guns from those who didn't want to hand them over.

Our door opened, and they demanded the same from us.

"You can see," said my mother to the man who spoke, "that we are too poor to have weapons."

"Nothing here. It's only women. And you, old man," he said to Raoul, "do you have a pistol?"

"I don't have any more weapons. I've already handed them over."

As soon as they went down the stairs, the house went quiet under the avalanche of clattering sabots and steel shoes. The invaders understood that they'd get nothing good from our household, and they left quickly, thinking that they'd have more luck elsewhere. They closed the door to our entryway. It was pointless.

The cavalry returned. This time it purposefully headed down our side of the street. The soldiers charged with sabers out. Furious shouts echoed among the crowd.

"The throats of the citizens are slit! Our brothers are massacred! Into the houses! Into the houses!"

At this signal, the doors were forced open. They came in through the shops, through the alleys. In less than an hour, the roofs along the docks were swarming with insurgents. The most horrifying were the children of twelve or fifteen. They'd made slings with straps of leather. Others who'd made their shirts into sacks for ammunition climbed to the tops of the pointed stone roofs armed with the pebbles that had paved the streets. They used the slings to send projectiles over far distances. Each stone that fell into a crowd wounded or killed a man. Some people aimed at the windows. If they didn't have weapons, the rioters threw anything they found out the windows. I still remember a parrot that they tossed, in its cage, from the second story of a house. For the next half hour, the sounds of its anguished cries could be heard above the chaos.

Our house was so advantageously located, from a military standpoint, that it was occupied from top to bottom. The fire in the street had blown in all the windows. We were more dead than alive. They came to wreck M. Raoul's workshop and scavenge wood from it. Raoul and his wife wept. They were ruined! Part of our poor household suffered the same losses.

After several hours of fighting, the conflict seemed to calm down. Eventually it died down completely. But this would be, as one might expect, a truce that lasted only a few hours.

My mother took advantage of this break. "Come on," she said, taking my hand. "Tomorrow this quarter will be burned to the ground. We need to get to Mathieu's place. It's out of the way. The riot won't have arrived there yet."

It was nearly nighttime. Going down the stairs, my foot slipped on something slick, and I fell flat on my back. I got up, and we went down a few more stairs to a place that was better lit. My mother let out a scream: I was covered in curdled black blood. The first-floor tenant had been killed. The blood had run under his door, and I had fallen in the puddle.

A group of armed rioters guarded the door. My

mother strode up to them. "Monsieurs," she said, "I must leave this house. I want to take refuge with friends. A woman and child cannot help in events like this. There's no one in the house. Look—death has stained this innocent child, and it has bloodied my dress."

"Are you going far?" he asked in a raspy voice.

"No, a hundred steps from here."

"We can escort you most of the way. Let's go, men!" And he turned to two of his comrades who were sitting on straw bales.

The four of us walked without saying a word. When we were in sight of a military encampment, the two men stopped.

"I can't go any farther," said one. "We don't want to walk into the jaws of the wolf."

"Thank you," said my mother. "You may leave us."

They turned on their heels without looking at us.

My mother found an officer, who provided two soldiers to accompany us. Our new escorts reassured us, and we liked them better. At Mathieu's door, my mother thanked the guards.

The family was in the middle of dinner. Everyone cried out upon seeing us come in. My mother told them everything that had happened. From the part of the city where Mathieu lived, you couldn't hear a thing. We knew there was still fighting, but the noise of the bullets didn't reach this quarter. The days that followed were bloody, but we were glad to not have to witness the riot.

❧

Calm had resettled on the city for a while when we received a letter from the mayor with an invitation for my mother to come to his office the next day. This letter was very intriguing.

"What could they want to see me about?" she kept asking.

My curiosity was no less aroused. I wanted to go with her, but she absolutely refused to take me.

She returned, out of breath, after half an hour.

"What happened?" asked M. Mathieu. "You are frighteningly pale, as if you ran."

"Oui, I ran, because—you don't know? My friends, my good friends, my husband is dead!"

"Your husband is dead! Good riddance!" cried M. Mathieu. My stepfather's behavior certainly justified this outburst from M. Mathieu. Nevertheless, Maman made no sign of agreement—maybe due to her manners, maybe because her heart, despite G…'s wrongs, was less harsh toward him than her head. "But my dear Jeanne, how did you come by this news?"

"I'll tell you the whole story. When I went into the mayor's office, he said, 'Are you the wife of G…?' 'Oui, monsieur.' And since I thought that he was going to speak to me of the theft that G… took part in, I became very pale. He saw this and said in a kind voice, 'Take hold of yourself, madame. What I have to tell you is tough, but you must be brave. Who is not called to experience such things in their life? Everyone is mortal.' I didn't understand at all. I promised to be brave, and I asked him to explain plainly.

"He began again: 'You have not seen your husband for some days?' 'Non, monsieur.' 'That's good. He was found at the Red Cross, hit by two bullets to the head. Here are the papers found on him: a wallet with his address and several letters not addressed to him, in a folder along with his passport.' I took the papers. There was no doubt G… no longer existed. The mayor spoke to me for some time, but I didn't hear a thing. And I ran to tell you the big news."

This changed everything for my mother. She was free. Nothing was keeping her from returning to Paris, which she planned to do, seeing as her little household had been sacked during the insurrection. She announced her intention to Mathieu. The family was sorry to see her go, but they didn't try to dissuade her.

That evening, when we were alone in our room, my mother said a long prayer to ask for grace for those no longer with us.

A few days later, we left Lyon. Since I no longer had to dread the presence of G…, it seemed as if nothing could cast a shadow on my happiness. I didn't know that life is often only a string of misfortunes and deceptions, and that further cruel suffering was in store for me.

5.

MONSIEUR VINCENT

I SHOULD STOP HERE. YOU are too indulgent in encouraging me to continue a story that thrives only on your interest. When I tell you, *My life is over!* you give me hope. When I tell you, *I'm bored!* you seek to reveal an intelligence I didn't know I had, one that maybe misery and misfortune had prevented at birth, or maybe because the kind of life I led was circumscribed.

※

As soon as we arrived in Paris, we had to go to my grandfather's house. It was very troubling for Maman. Her father had remarried after divorcing his first wife, and Maman did not like her stepmother. She was a horrid woman who hated the children from her husband's first marriage and treated them very badly.

There were three of them: two girls and a boy. They

had enthusiastically learned their trades in order to be able to leave as soon as they could support themselves. The house held the memory of their mother, who had been replaced by a stranger and made their home unbearable.

Adèle, the oldest daughter, was in the house of a lace merchant. She came to a sad end. One evening at about ten o'clock, she was carrying a carton of lace spindles that were worth an enormous sum down rue de la Lune. A man assaulted her and stabbed her three times: first in the cheek, which cut her tongue; second in her chest; and third in her side. There was a woman in a nearby doorway who went to fetch a man to save Adèle. Her assailant had a long overcoat, and his hat covered his eyes. He fled, yelling, "Goddamn it, I made a mistake."

The victim was taken to the hospital, where she died some hours later of the wound in her side, without anyone even knowing her name. It was only some time later that they knew where she belonged, thanks to the carton of lace, which had been taken to the police station. The perpetrator of the crime was never found.

My mother was placed with a hatmaker, while her brother went to learn to paint.

The stepmother was happy. The children were far away, and they gave up on the idea of coming to visit. Whenever they stopped by to see their father, they were received so coldly that they didn't bother to come back anymore.

Besides, my grandfather had a certain preference for his son. Though he fought about it with his wife, my grandfather made him more welcome than his sisters and even gave him gifts in secret. My grandfather's mind was going, which the painter took advantage of.

Once when they didn't want to give him any money, he returned to their house with two pistols. He said to his father and stepmother, "I want some money; I know it's here. Open the desk, or I'll blow your brains out." They gave him what was in the desk, plus the silverware. He was on his way out when he stopped in the middle of the staircase and laughed like an insane man. "I fooled you both," he called out. "These pistols aren't loaded." He left France, and they didn't see him again for years.

My mother took on her trade and established herself without asking anything from her father. She could not forgive him the wrong he had done to their mother. I think that in twelve years, she'd only seen him twice. I know she took me there once a year for a while. My personality was apparent early on. I love passionately or I hate furiously; I'm never in the middle. I adore my mother, but I sobbed when we had to see my grandfather. The idea of hugging him kept me up at night.

I still felt this way when we went to his house upon our arrival from Lyon. We arrived at ten o'clock in the evening, no. 8 rue de Bercy-Saint-Jean. This was more an arcade than a street. My grandfather's house was one of the finest on the street. His shop sold furniture, and we could read the sign from two feet away: Furnished house kept by …. Furniture old and new bought and sold. You entered by a door so narrow that you could only pass through by turning sideways. A half door decorated with a bell announced people coming and going, which was pointless, because my grandfather (he said it was to save money, I said it was stinginess) was the proprietor, porter, house boy, and furniture seller all by himself.

His apartment was on the first floor. I like to live in the finest lodgings, but he *had* to. He had a pass-through from his shop. The place was lovely, with two huge casement windows and a balcony with an iron railing eaten away by rust. It was at the end of the street, which was so narrow that you could touch hands with the person across the way.

It was into this place that we entered, hearts clenched, heads bowed, so sure were we of the poor welcome that we would receive.

The room opened off the shop. There was so much furniture, plus pendulum clocks, and paintings, and overwhelming luxury that it was hard to know where to sit.

My grandfather was seated in a comfortable armchair. The bell had alerted him; he turned his head and said with all the sangfroid in the world, "At last, it's you, my girl. What the hell are you doing here at this hour? We're about to go to bed." He hadn't seen us for two years.

"Father, I arrived just now from Lyon. I came to ask if I could stay for a day or two."

The stepmother leaped from her chair and said in her nasal voice, "We don't have an available room. It's too bad."

"That's true," said my grandfather. "We could make a bed for you on the floor."

My mother told them everything that had brought us there. The stepmother pretended she'd fallen asleep.

Maman said to her father, "I have a lot of other things to tell you when we are alone."

The stepmother pretended to wake up and said in the sweetest voice, "Goodnight. I'm going to bed." Then she went into the next room, being sure to leave the door ajar.

My grandfather got up and closed it. Coming back

to his chair, he said to my mother, "Well, my girl, what do you intend to do?"

"What I always do: work, with a place to live included in my employment. Tomorrow I'll look for lodgings. If you would furnish it for me, I will pay you as soon as possible."

"Certainly, I'll give you what you need, but only to keep the peace. There's no need for her to suspect anything." He looked toward the door. He must have been afraid he'd been heard, because he began talking more quietly. "Do you have any money?"

"No, I had to pay the full fare for my daughter, the trip is long, and my funds are exhausted."

He pulled a handful of keys from his pocket, opened a drawer very quietly, took out a bag, and handed it to my mother. "Here, put this in your trunk. There are a hundred écus; that will help you. But not a word in front of her!"

✦

My mother spent the next day out of the house. She found lodgings near the Temple and the canal. She stopped in, and it was available, so the next day we moved in.

A few days later, she went to some manufacturers that she knew, who consigned her to do enough piecework to keep a few hired workers busy. I worked with her. Sundays we went for a walk in the park, or sometimes she took me to see a show. My mother never went so far as the end of the street without me. No one else ever loved me. I didn't have friends like the other children. The things I had seen left me with too deep a sadness.

I was eight and a half, but I was tall, skinny, pale. I

could have passed for twelve. I was jealous of anyone my mother seemed to like even a little. If she went out without me, I would make myself sick.

Below us was a sculptor who sang from morning to night. M. Vincent seemed to be about thirty-five, with short blond hair and blue eyes that were neither large nor small and were kind but expressionless. He had a well-formed nose with wide nostrils, a round face, and a smallish mouth with full lips and fine teeth. His shoulders were broad and his neck short; he was about five feet, three or four inches tall. He had a fresh complexion, but it was hard to say if that was due to the stone dust smeared all over it. He was happy as a finch. Everyone called him the jester.

I ran all the errands for my mother, and I met the sculptor almost every day on the stairs. He laughed with me. He seemed like the best guy in the world.

One day he said to me, "My little girl, you should tell madame your mother to let you come to my studio for an hour to pose for a bust."

I told him I didn't know what posing for a bust was, and that he should ask Maman. I didn't have to tell him twice. He was at our place before I'd made it to the top of the stairs. He'd already explained, it seemed, and my mother answered, "I would like that very much."

He and I became the best friends in the world. He was always at our place. He had the gift of making friends with everyone he saw. He was neither handsome nor ugly, but he was kind beyond all expectation. He was no great wit, but very glib. He had one fault: he was a playboy. When a woman to his liking passed in the street, he followed her the entire day. The wealthy, the workers, the wives of friends, the pretty, the ugly, the old, the young—he knocked on all their doors. When they spoke to him, he said, "When the dog's off his leash, he has the right to run."

He was one of those people who bore you sometimes but who become indispensable.

His mother came to his place often. He drove her mad. She would come down to see us, and once she invited us to dinner. After that, he and my mother no longer moved one without the other. My mother was less kind to me. I became so jealous that I spied on them constantly, and they hid from me. I saw what was going on clearly—my brain worked. I became spiteful. I didn't eat. I was vicious, and I paid for it. Really, I was awful.

When we went for a walk and M. Vincent wanted to take my mother's arm, I threw myself between them and latched onto her. I said, "Maman, I beg of you."

She looked at me in astonishment and walked with me alone, but this bored her.

M. Vincent was courteous to me, as G… had been at first. But, as with G…, it didn't work. If he served me at the table, I didn't eat.

I suffered so much, and I became so hateful, that I couldn't hold it together anymore. I asked my mother to find an apprenticeship for me. I told her that I would learn a trade. The very next day, she told me that the following Monday, I would go to M. Grange, rue de Temple.

"Your employer," she said, "has a daughter about your age. You'll do very well."

This was a mortal wound to my heart, seeing how quickly she got rid of me. I was still proud; I did not shed a tear.

Monday came. My mother took me to M. Grange's. I had never seen anything so ugly as this man! I had never seen anyone as pretty as his daughter! She was short, with reddish-blonde hair, fair and fresh, fashionable and elegant, almost fifteen years old. I was by this time eleven, yet I was taller than her. I had a forest of very dark hair, and I had light skin. It was the contrast people remarked on the most.

M. Grange asked my mother if she wanted me to lodge there. Before she had time to answer, I said, "Yes, let me sleep here, that would be least inconvenient for you."

My mother said angrily, "Of course not, mademoiselle. You shall come home every day." This was the first time in my life that she had been formal with me.

I left in the morning and only came back in the evening, never returning home at the same time. Often Maman had gone out and came back late. I would wait in the street when I didn't want to go to bed. I could have stayed in the shop, but I wasn't happy there.

The daughter of my employer ran the place. She had the keys to everything. She stole from the till to buy herself things, but M. Grange didn't even notice. This child, who had lost her mother very young, had always been spoiled. It was heartbreaking.

She found great pleasure in humiliating me, in saying embarrassing things to me. She wasn't good at anything, while I was more capable than the best worker. Nevertheless, the daughter sometimes threw my work in

74

my face, saying, "Undo this. It's badly made." My teeth clenched, my heart raced, and a cloud passed before my eyes. I struggled to breathe. I waited five minutes, then I unraveled my work without saying a word. Enraged as I was, I could not scream or break something. I could only cry to soothe myself. But as I would rather have died than shed a tear in front of her, I was sick with rage.

There were ten ateliers in this building. In the evening during the summer, the workers would gather on the doorstep. If we were all chatting, the daughter would tell me, "Go home. Your mother's waiting." Everyone in the building noticed her harshness toward me, and they pitied me for being her scapegoat. I remained patient, telling myself that it would be the same anywhere else—maybe even worse.

My apprenticeship ended, and I asked M. Grange if he wanted to keep me on as a day worker.

"Certainly. I'll give you twenty sous a day, and if, when your day is done, there's a rush job, you would have it." He looked at his daughter. "I can see you're upset, Louisa. You can't tell her off; she's a woman. How old are you, Céleste?"

"I just turned fourteen."

"Well, I thought you were much older. You're strong." Then he turned away from me and spent the next six months not looking at me.

The shop shared the courtyard with a maker of marbled papers. The office clerk there was always in the shop or at the door. My boss's daughter left when she noticed him, and she reddened when he went back in. I thought this was a childish crush. She was seventeen, he eighteen.

One day the paper maker came to my station and

watched as I worked. We used a lot of gold trimming on our velvet. I did all of the embroidery, and I was told I was very skilled at it. My young employer came over, mad as a wet hen. She reddened all the way to her hair.

"That's badly done," she said. "Don't finish it. No one will want it."

I looked at my stitching and said with a laugh, "You can't be serious. You take footbaths to calm your skin, and it's apparently all for nothing. You're as red as a poppy. If that was all, fine, but you're talking about something you know nothing about. I could never even teach you to braid the trim." I handed my piece to another worker. She'd been in the shop for ten years and treated Louisa like a child.

"Céleste's work is well done," she said. "Good of you to give advice to others, when you aren't good at anything."

I watched Louisa and nearly felt sorry for her. I thought her head was going to explode. Her eyes popped like lottery balls. She stood for a minute with her mouth open and looked so stupid that I was almost avenged for all she'd done to me. I had nothing to lose by waiting.

She hid herself in the back of the shop, and when her father came in, she began to sob hot tears, saying that I was mean to her. M. Grange said he didn't believe it at all and that it was more likely me who was the victim.

That same evening, when I went home, I found my mother very upset. M. Vincent hadn't come by since the day before. My mother did all she could not to cry, but it was easy to see she suffered in his absence. When M. Vincent came in without knocking, my mother welcomed him coldly.

I'd had a good day, and I went to bed content. My

heart, which had such need of affection, became full of hate. All the tenderness I'd once had toward my mother had dried up. I felt unknown impulses inside myself. My imagination became more independent, more daring. Instead of sleeping, I spent hours looking at the stars. My thoughts followed the passing clouds, and I stood as if in ecstasy. I saw myself as rich, happy, loved.

The theaters, where I'd been taken when I was young, had spoiled my mind and kindled my character. I can assure you that I don't know anything more dangerous for children than this kind of distraction.

Vincent ate at our house. He only went to his studio to work. And so drama quickly followed.

Whenever he said a word to me, I answered, "Mind your own business. Do I have to know about it? You're not my parent."

My mother demanded I keep quiet.

"Fine," I said to her. "I know you don't love me, that I'm an embarrassment, an annoyance. If I were old enough, I'd leave. I'd rent a little room where I would be alone."

"Be patient," she said.

I was making myself hated, but the feeling was stronger than me.

❧

We often went to M. Vincent's mother's. One evening when I came home, I was told by the building's concierge that my mother was at rue Popincourt, where Mme Vincent lived. I went to join them. Mme Vincent told me to wait, that my mother and M. Vincent would return soon.

We both fell asleep, me on a chaise, she in an armchair. When I woke up, the gaslight was low.

"It must be very late," I said, rubbing my eyes. "They haven't returned. I'll go."

It was after midnight. It was cold. There were few houses along the canal, only some launderers. At the water's edge, squares of wood were piled up to dry. The few lights were spaced very far apart.

I stopped at the corner of rue Popincourt. I didn't dare go any farther. The street seemed built to scare even people braver than me. I told myself that they would be worried about me at home, that maybe they'd gone on ahead of me, that I would meet them halfway up the street. I followed along the docks. I hugged the walls breathlessly. I was not very heavy; I walked like a bird so no one could hear my footsteps.

When I was almost to the Ménilmontant bridge, I heard talking. I stopped, and without knowing why, I hid in a doorway. I didn't hear footsteps; my eyes sought to pierce the night. The voices started up again. They moved as they spoke. I thought at first they were in a boat, since it seemed as if they were coming from the water. But then I heard feet stomping on the ground. They were next to the canal, behind piles of wood. Finally I distinctly heard pleading.

"Don't hurt me. I told you that's all I had."

"That's not true," said another person in a whisper. "You got paid. Today is Saturday."

"No, I swear, I'm paid every two weeks."

"That's not true."

I heard a different footstep on the ground, then two or three groans, and something fell.

"Quick, search him," said the man who had already

spoken.

"There's nothing," answered the other. "You didn't have to kill him."

"Shut up! He would have busted us. You're so smart, you are!"

I heard something fall in the water. I slid to my knees in the corner of the doorway. I shrouded my head with my black smock so that my white cap wouldn't attract their attention, and I gave my soul to God. Footsteps were approaching. I lost consciousness.

When I came to, I was still very afraid. I was in a huge room lit by five or six lamps hanging from the wall by the hooks of their iron candlesticks, huge vats that smoked, and braziers whose fire illuminated these vats. The fumes poured out in a cloud, and shadows shifted among them, but I was unable to distinguish anything.

A large woman came up to me and said, "Well, you feel better?"

I threw myself backward.

"Do I scare you, my child?"

"Oui, madame."

"Don't be afraid, I won't hurt you." She began to laugh so kindly that I began to feel a little reassured. "What were you doing out there at this hour?"

I still wasn't awake enough to remember what had happened. I looked at her sideways and said, "Where, out there?"

"There, in the doorway of our laundry, of course! When we came to put the detergent in, we found you laid out on your side."

"Ah! I remember...close your door—hurry! Hurry! They're still there!"

"Who are?"

I told them what I'd heard.

"Poor girl," she said, "no wonder you were scared! A drowned man—that's not rare around here."

Someone took a candle and went to the edge of the canal. There was no trace of the fight, and they didn't even find the place where the unlucky man had died.

I was taken back to my mother's. Knowing that I had been at Mme Vincent's, she thought that I'd stayed there. I was deathly cold; my teeth chattered. The doctor said he believed I had typhoid fever. He wasn't wrong.

I was sick for two months. My grief was present the entire time, because I could no longer doubt it: my mother loved M. Vincent to the point that nothing was left over for me.

❦

I went back to work, but in order to get home every day, I had to cross the canal. The Temple bridge was busy. This didn't stop me from having fears I could not master. I would arrive at the house out of breath and ashen, then spend an hour wandering about without anyone getting a word out of me. It was believed that the sight of this house made me ill, so my mother made plans to move.

At first I thought this was solely for my benefit, and I was very grateful. I thought that by leaving this house, we would cut ourselves loose from all the people who lodged there. I was wrong. M. Vincent came along with us, and if my mother left the quarter, it was mostly to get away from all the things those women knew about him.

My hate grew stronger. I said to myself, *If only it had been him who'd been thrown into the canal! I miss G....*

I tried another strategy: spying on Vincent. He didn't

hide anything, and besides, it wasn't difficult to find out what he was doing. I believe he loved my mother very much, but it was impossible for him to be faithful to her. My mother was jealous of these women in the wings. I knew that I wanted her to know.

During dinner I said to Vincent, "I have to say, your new girlfriend is not pretty. You shouldn't be running after her anyway; she doesn't want you."

He became red, my mother white. They fought for days. When they made up, I lost even more of my affection for my mother.

❧

One day, my shop arranged a trip to the countryside for the workers. Everyone went—men, women, children. M. Grange paid for it, and so I went without asking permission.

My mother lost her temper and hit me harder than usual. She was irate; I was stubborn. I often got slapped. Vincent came to my defense and stepped in front of me. But I didn't want to owe him anything, so I took the blows.

Finally, after being slapped enough times, I said to my mother, "It's all well and good for you to judge my morals and tell me that I conducted myself shamefully when I went to the country with my friends—along with my employer and his daughter, and my fellow workers, who like me more than you do. I guess I've gotten used to being alone. If I wanted to do something bad, it's not your supervision that would stop me. No one would say a word about it. The people at the shop often say that you set a bad example for me."

I was far enough away from her. She looked at me with frightening eyes. Vincent seemed stunned. I leaned against the wall. I waited to be knocked out, but I was resigned to it. I had tended my broken heart for too long.

On the table beside my mother there was a small knife with a pearl handle. It was always there; Vincent had given it to me. She threw it at my face. In the Middle Ages, I think they called this move "tirer à l'oie," to kill by the eye. She aimed true. Luckily the handle was much heavier than the blade. Instead of slashing my flesh and bursting my eye, the knife cut my left eyebrow.

Blood covered my face. My mother realized what she'd done and sobbed. She came to her senses. I had a scratch that would only leave a scar.

Vincent growled at her. She wanted to make me forget what she'd done with her tenderness, her kisses. But it was too late. My heart was closed off to her attention, which had previously filled it up. It wasn't because I'd been slapped or cut; my mother could have killed me for all I cared. I had to carry on in pain. I knew that if she'd become violent, if her hand had turned against me, she wouldn't think twice anymore. She'd sacrificed me for love. Instead of keeping me in her confidence, in her affections, she had allowed my awful instincts to take over without fighting to correct them.

My imagination was aflame. I harbored so much hate I wished death on those I detested.

❧

If I had at this time any way to educate myself, I believe that I would have been better off. Sadly my desire for knowledge surpassed the resources I had for learning, and I barely knew how to read.

I defied everyone. I took my mother's turn against me as a sneer. I became colder, more uncaring, more independent. I was fifteen. I was often told that I was very pretty.

Louisa had become ugly. She had lovers; this didn't help. Her greatest feature had been her youthfulness. She was irritated to see that, without my seeking them, I was getting looks and compliments.

My mother, Vincent, and I had changed lodgings; we were now at no. 23 rue Neuve-Culture-Saint-Catherine. It was a detached house on the corner. The windows overlooked rue Culture, but we could see Saint Paul's church and the rue Saint-Antoine from our place. The entryway was oddly built. The front stairs ended at the street; someone had certainly wanted to take advantage of the location. There was only one shop that took up the entire bottom floor, occupied by a wine merchant.

Our lodgings were on the second floor, and we had three rooms: a kitchen, a large bedroom with an alcove, and another bedroom without a fireplace that was lit by a half-glass door that closed and locked. It was really a large closet, but the proprietor in his vanity had called it a bedroom, and I, in much the same way, also called it my bedroom. A muslin curtain had been hung over the glass door, which did not keep me from seeing everything that went on in my mother's room.

M. Vincent had given up on being a sculptor. He had gotten an office job. He stayed at our house, so this was our household. Despite all I'd done to him, he was fine. He seemed to like me more each day. He gave me gifts, was friendly, and spent more time with me than with my mother.

One night after I went to bed, I heard him say to Maman, "I'm telling you, this isn't wise. You must take her back to the shop with you. She'll be fifteen soon, she's pretty, and those locusts are running after her."

My mother answered, "You know very well it's not up to me. She doesn't want to leave her job. Could I have done anything about the way she is? I would shut her in, but that would only make her sulk. I don't dare say a word to her anymore; she says nasty things to me because of you."

"There are always ways to force a girl to stay in her mother's house. I will take over watching her. I don't want her to turn bad."

My mother told Vincent he was insane, that if he seemed to be watching me, he would make me flee the house. They spoke of me for a long time, always in the same way. But since the subject never changed, I ended up falling asleep.

❧

My grandfather had been affected by a frightening illness they called scurvy. He went to Fontainebleu to stay with one of his brothers. He was feeling so sick that he wrote to my mother to ask her to come sit with him. My mother went, putting me in charge of the household.

I came home, as usual, every evening. M. Vincent came in very late.

Two or three times, I awoke with a start. He was near my bed, a lamp in his hand.

"What do you want?" I asked.

"Nothing. I was watching you sleep. I have to keep an eye on you while your mother is away. They notice you in the courtyard. Do you know that you're almost of age to marry? That would be very lucky for you." Then he stepped back and looked at me, his eyes shining in the light. This scared me without my knowing quite why. I hid in my bed as if my comforter were a castle wall.

Soon he received a letter from my mother. He told me my grandfather was very ill and that my mother would stay with him another week or so.

I came home that evening in tears. I had fought with Louisa. I had been less patient with the social niceties, and I got carried away. Her father took her side. It was unfair. I asked for my pay, and I was given it. I was without a job.

"Why do you torment yourself?" Vincent asked. "Aren't I here for you? Let me take care of you. I love you, though you detest me. I would do everything for you."

He took me in his arms and kissed me many times. Little by little, he squeezed himself so close to me that I felt his rapid heartbeat. I wanted to escape, but he held me.

"No, stay. That's when you really know someone loves you." His breath was hot on my face, and his lips trembled.

I didn't say anything. I rushed into my room.

"What are you doing?" he said.

"Nothing," I answered, because I didn't know why I'd run away.

He'd known me as a child. He was still in the habit of speaking to me like a little girl.

I returned ashamed, and I sat near the window. He came over to sit by me.

"You're so mad at me that you take off whenever I come near you! You're jealous of me because of your mother. You're completely wrong, because without you, I wouldn't have come around to see her so much."

I looked at him, stunned.

He took my hand and went on. "I am a cad; I love women. But until this day, I was incapable of loving the same woman for long. You—I can't leave you." He looked me in the eyes and squeezed my hand.

I glanced behind me as if looking for my mother. I don't know why, but I wanted her to hear him.

"You're kidding yourself," I answered. "I was never jealous. I hate you because my mother loves you more than she loves me. If you stayed because of me, you have been sorely mistaken. I want you to leave. I would be glad to never see you again."

He seemed dumbfounded. I took advantage of this to tell him that it was very late and I was going to my room.

Since he hadn't kept his lamp lit, I extinguished mine and got undressed in the dark.

❧

I spent the next day at home. Two men came to ask Vincent to dinner; they left their names with me. Vincent came in around three in the afternoon. I gave him what they'd written down, and he went out to find them.

I only had two dresses, and I spent the day mending my things. At ten that night, I was still working. I had removed what I'd been wearing to repair the hem. I was in a slip and chemise, with a scarf around my neck, when I heard knocking. I put a shawl over my shoulders and went to open the door. Vincent entered.

He didn't look himself. From the first words he said

to me, I knew that he was drunk.

"You have made a conquest already," he said. "They spoke kindly of you at dinner. The shorter one told me that you're his type. I answered that the oven wasn't warming up for him, that I'm keeping you."

"What? You're keeping me? Do you think I'm not ever going to marry?" I stumbled back a step. "I very much hope that you don't ask me. You love me as your daughter, and I'm thankful for that, but you can't marry your daughter." I looked into his eyes because I wanted to know what he was thinking. My heart skipped a beat.

I looked toward the door. It was locked. Usually the key was left in the lock, but the door was bolted closed. I saw, between the strike plate and the lock, that he had given it two turns and taken the key. I was scared. He was out of his mind. He came near me.

Within a minute, ten different ideas came to mind. I wanted to ask for his mercy or to threaten to kill him if he touched me. Calling on all my courage, I drew my shawl tightly around me and said, looking him right in the face, "What do you want from me?"

He hesitated an instant, holding his arms out for me to take, and answered in a husky voice, "I want you to love me! I want to have you! I will have you!"

I ran to the door; it was locked. I wrapped my arms around myself. I told him that I was going to scream for help if he touched me. He took me by the waist and clasped me in his arms.

I tried so hard to slide to the ground that I managed to do it, and clinging to the wooden bedpost with all my might, I yelled for help. My voice was weak. He pulled off my shawl and ripped my camisole. Modesty and shame made me loosen my grip on the bed. I crossed my arms to hide my nearly naked chest.

He picked me up and held me, saying, "Shut up! Give yourself willingly, or I will take you by force."

I couldn't move at all. He pinned my arms to my sides. His head bent toward my shoulder, and I felt his wet mouth. I shivered in fear and disgust. I felt damned.

I struggled uselessly. Then, with a spark of inspiration, I bit his arm so hard that he yelled and released me.

I ran to the window, opened it, and climbed onto the sill. "If you come near me, I'll throw myself out." I had decided to die.

He understood and backed off. "Fine! I won't touch you anymore, just come down."

"No," I said. "You leave. I will come down then."

He asked me to forgive him and told me it was a moment of madness. I could come down, and he would promise not to do it again. It was not my confidence in his word that made me decide to leave my perch; it was the black abyss I saw that frightened me. Having been pushed to the edge, I would have jumped. But I had time to reconsider, and the instinct to live was reawakened in me—along with fear. Nevertheless, I stayed near the window.

He again threw himself upon me and held me by my slip and my arms. He said, trying to keep me away from the window, "You think that I'll leave if you say anything about this. But I'll tell your mother that you tempted me. She'll believe it, because she is jealous and she loves me."

I began to scream. He grabbed me so brutally that my body slumped over toward the open window and my elbow smashed a pane of glass. I didn't feel it at all, but it made noise in the street, which scared Vincent. He flew from the room, leaving the door open.

I found three cuts on my arms. I took my dress, my shawl, and a cap, and I left the house without knowing where I was going.

In the middle of the stairway, fear overcame me again. I didn't dare descend one step farther. There was no concierge in this building. The stairway wasn't lit. The door to the street opened with a key; it seemed to me as if it had been locked on purpose. I went back up the stairs like a shadow, and I stopped at the floor below mine.

I heard someone going up. Our door was open. It stayed open, and I saw a ray of light coming through the crack.

If he finds me, I said to myself, *he'll kill me. I need to get out of this house*. I threw myself into the darkness with alarming speed. If he wanted to try to stop me, I thought, I would scream so loudly it would bring the whole world to see. But this idea didn't give me a whole lot of courage, because there were only two renters in our house, one on the fourth floor and us on the second.

I passed by our door as I again went downstairs. The ray of light from the open door hit me. I thought Vincent was going to attack me like a wolf. I hurled myself toward the first floor. I didn't hear anything.

Once on the ground floor, I pushed on the door, and I walked along the edge of the place Royal. I came back along rue Saint-Antoine. The bells of Saint Paul rang out two in the morning. I reentered the street via the rue Culture; I slid along the buildings.

I saw the light in our window. What was he doing? Why did he come back? He hadn't seen me leave. He must have believed I'd either disappeared or died. Maybe he was waiting for me to return? Maybe he had run after me?

I didn't have to think about it too long. I saw him look out the window, and I hid behind some scaffolding.

This quarter has always been very gloomy, but during this era, everything closed up at ten in the evening. I crossed the way and ensconced myself in the garage door of the grain merchant next door to our building.

Tell me why, having so many reasons to be afraid, I came so close to being found. I have no idea myself.

I had walked for two hours.

The plant and grain merchant had his shop at the back of the courtyard. The granary where he kept his straw and hay was on the first floor. I pressed myself against his door. Someone had forgotten to latch it. I went in and fixed that mistake.

Once the door was closed behind me, I could breathe. I felt the fear of finding oneself alone at fifteen, in the streets of Paris, friendless and without knowing anyone you could ask to take you in, because my mother had sacrificed all of her friends for Vincent.

My head was spinning. Between fatigue and the late hour, I felt my eyes closing in spite of myself. I walked down the hallway and found the stairs to the hayloft. I went up a few steps to sit and collect myself. The door to the loft was open, so I went in. I stretched out on the bales of hay and slept until the first light of day.

6.

THÉRÈSE

hat to do? I SAID to myself on waking and shivering with cold. I couldn't go back to our place. My mother had written five days before that she'd be back in a week, which meant she'd be back tomorrow or the next day. I would wait for her. I would tell her everything, and we'd be together again. But what to do for two days? I could take long walks and come back here at night. If I was spotted, I would tell the truth. I had ten sous; that was more than enough while I waited for her to return. I didn't want to say anything to anyone.

I spent the first day on the docks watching men fish. I spent two sous on bread.

Five days passed this way; my mother did not return.

I wept. I was hungry. I could no longer walk while I waited for it to be late enough to go back to the granary.

I sat on the steps of Saint Paul, holding my head in my hands, and I asked God if it wouldn't be better if I just threw myself in the water. Lots of people passed by without looking at me. Then I felt someone tap my shoulder.

"What are you doing here, dear? You've been here for more than two hours. Are you crying?" The person who spoke was a woman of twenty-five or thirty, with quite a pretty face. She wore a black silk dress, a beribboned cap, and an apron with colorful flowers (as was the fashion). She held her dress up on one side, letting a well-shod foot in a black bootie show. Her very white, very close-fitting stockings spoke of her elegance and spotlessness.

I liked her face. She didn't have to ask me the same thing twice—I told her why I was there. She moved us into a narrow space between the shops and the church. It was dim; she seemed to want to avoid being seen.

"Poor girl," she said. "Do you think your mother will be back soon?"

"I hope so. Tomorrow, maybe the day after, but she can't be later than that."

She asked if I could write. I said that I didn't know how, and that in any case I didn't know my mother's address in Fontainebleu.

She hesitated. "You can't sleep in the street, and I can't take you in. Well, whatever. You have to eat. Here's the thing: I can't walk beside you. Follow a few steps behind me. When you see me enter a house, enter after me."

I was so afraid of losing her that I walked at her heels. I saw her laugh with women who paced back and forth on the street. One of them said as we passed, "Are you going back to the house? You're being followed."

"Oui," she said, and looking at me, she began to laugh good-naturedly.

After about two hundred feet, she stopped in front of the door of a wine merchant and glanced into the shop. There were a lot of people inside.

She went into an entryway that had red curtains beside the shop and signaled for me to wait. She opened a door that should have given onto one of the wine merchant's rooms, then took a candle and a long key with a number carved on it. At the first floor, she opened a glass door hung with red calico curtains, like those of the wine merchant. The room had a low ceiling, a bed, a sofa, two chairs, and a table.

"Go in," she said to me, "don't be afraid. You're hungry; you must eat. Tomorrow, I'm going to see if your mother has returned. You'll sleep better here than in the street."

I wanted to cling to her neck, but I was nervous about the noise coming from the other side of the wall, at the wine merchant's. She returned with bread, wine, and cured meats. I ate. I was so hungry that my stomach knotted, and I was ill.

"Well!" she said. "Does that feel better?"

"Oui, madame, thank you so much. I would like to stay with you. You seem so kind. I want to kiss you." She offered me her cheek, and I kissed it with all my heart.

I asked her what she did. She answered, "What do I do! I would be doing wrong to take you under my wing. I was like you—a man treated me the same way one wanted to treat you six days ago. I couldn't defend myself, and here's where I ended up."

"Are you sick?" I said, astonished.

"No—not today, anyway! You make me very happy, and I would be glad to see you again."

"Why couldn't you?"

"Don't ask. I have to hide that you're here in order to keep you safe for a day or two. If anyone knew you were here, people would suspect things I don't want to even think about—though not about you. All kinds of harm would come to me. How old are you?"

"I just turned fifteen."

She leaped from her chair. "Fifteen!" she repeated. "Good God! I could get six months!"

"Six months!" I said without understanding.

"Oui, my girl. Corruption of a minor—at least six months."

"I don't understand."

"It's difficult to explain. I'm not a woman; I'm a number. I no longer operate by my own rule but by the rule of the card. If I want to go about bareheaded, the rule tells me to wear a hat. If I want to go out during the day, the rule forbids me. I cannot go down certain streets. I should never pose in windows, and above all I should not be seen with an honest woman. Think what it would be with a young girl of fifteen! They'd say I wanted to pimp you out."

"They'd ask me what was going on, though, right?"

"Maybe yes, but it's dangerous. Me, I live like this because I'm carefree…and also I don't have the means to leave this life. But I've never been arrested."

I just looked at her. This acknowledgment didn't bother me.

"Pay attention, dear, and never fall into vice! You see, I'd be sorry I didn't leave you to die of hunger. Your mother will kick this man out. Work and stay aboveboard;

you should be so lucky. Come on, go to bed, poor little one. Wait, here are clean clothes. You can give them back to me."

I had slept six nights without getting undressed. It was a joy that I cannot express to put on a white chemise and pass out. When I woke in the morning, I was surprised to find this woman nearby. I remembered all that had happened, and I thanked her anew.

She kept her word. That morning, toward ten o'clock, she went to my place and came back to tell me that my mother had not returned.

"Tomorrow, then," I said.

She promised to keep me another day or two if she had to. She left that evening and came back very late.

This went on for three days. I never saw anyone who didn't want to be seen.

∝∽∾

The third day, feeling that she could no longer put me up, she proposed taking me to Maman's stepmother, who was probably staying in their Paris house. I had thought of that, but I didn't dare go out of fear of hurting Maman when I told her what had happened. We were not far from it when two men approached us.

"What are your names?" said one.

She gave them names, but she became so pale that I thought she might faint.

"And that one," he said, gesturing at me, "is she registered?"

"Non, she's a poor girl who doesn't know where her mother is. I've hidden her for three days."

"How old is she?" he asked, coming near me.

"Fifteen," she answered, hesitating.

"Ah!" he said. "Have her follow us. We're going to take her. She'll be well taken care of in detention."

These words were a terrible blow.

She told them I was smart, and they began to laugh.

"I'm done for," she said to me quietly. "They're going to put me away for six months." She was so upset that she gave me a thousand pieces of advice, which she begged me not to forget. There went her freedom.

I was a little anxious when I saw that she was coming along with me. My anxiety became terror when I saw that they were taking me to the police station. I ran over to the Seine. I wanted to throw myself off the bridge. These men took pity on me and told me very kindly that I would leave the station the next day.

This poor woman advised me what to say, and I promised that I'd say all she asked.

We walked along the docks, then we came before an archway. We entered into a large courtyard. Our guide steered us toward a small door with iron bars and frosted panes of glass behind them. The man went up two steps, took the iron door knocker in hand, and knocked. The sound brought my heart back, as if I'd let it fall behind. We went into a square room.

To the right of the entrance was a desk behind a grille; that's where they took down your name. To the left, a strap bed where the guard slept. At the back, numbered passageways. The men who had brought us left.

"Over here," said a man who had a distinctive uniform. He had us follow him to the right. Everything was lit by an oil lamp.

I saw a door with glass panes behind the counter. The man opened it.

"You'll have company," he said as he closed the door behind us.

I found myself in an enormous room, which seemed to be a holding cell with cots along its length.

The bolts creaked, the door opened, and someone called my name, saying, "I made a mistake. There's one here for the littles' room."

I went out, and they had me go up three floors. A door was opened for me, and I was made to go into what they called the room for little girls. It was very dark. I thought that I was going to be alone. The floor was covered with mattresses; that's all I could see.

I heard a small voice say to me, "Hey, there's room for you. Stretch out over there."

I sat down without answering. I passed the night more afraid than you can imagine. I tried to see in the darkness. I was in an uncomfortable position. My eyes, tired from not being able to make anything out, burned like two embers. I had such vivid hallucinations that I lost track of myself. I sobbed and spoke incoherently.

Someone came over to me, took my head in their arms, and said, "Don't weep so. Tomorrow they'll come get you. Surely you have parents?"

I gave in to these kindnesses. I sighed and resigned myself to waiting for daybreak.

Time seemed so long! At last I could see black bars against pale blue about six feet up from the floor. It was a window two feet wide, eighteen inches tall, maybe more, with iron bars.

The room where I found myself was large, four meters square. The walls were painted a light color and covered with inscriptions made with the point of a knife. A heating pipe crossed the room a foot from the wall, below the opening that gave onto the hallway. A rickety wooden bench made up the furniture. In one corner, a pitcher of water, and in the other, a bucket.

The longest one could stay at the police station, as I would later learn, was a week. You can't leave the room for one second, and there can only be up to ten people in there at a time. The mattresses were made with sackcloth, the blankets with brown linen.

I had three fellow captives. I couldn't see the two women or girls who were at the rear of the room; their blankets covered them completely. I read the big white letters on my blanket: Prison Cell.

My heart clenched. I remembered the voice that, some hours before, had comforted me. I looked around. As soon as I did, I threw myself on the floor in terror. What was next to me was not a human form. It was bent in half. I could see two bare feet, black as ink, with long nails. What had served as a slip must have once been dark wool, but it was covered in mud and wrinkled, and the hem was ragged. A floral cotton blouse, faded and torn in the back, allowed me to see a dirty rag of an undershirt. All this was stained by bugs.

I hugged the wall and looked around. I did what anyone would do when you see something scratch itself: I rubbed my shoulders against the wall and expected to be devoured by vermin.

I'd always had a naughty mind, but I believed my heart was good. I remembered that this poor creature had said a kind word to me. I moved closer to look at her. Her head rested on her shoulder. Her auburn hair was dirty, and it fell in disarray around her neck and cheek, so I couldn't see her face.

I decided to wait, and I went to sit on the bench. I

thought of all that had happened to me. Sadness over-whelmed me, and I let myself go and cried. "My God! Have pity on me. Let me die." I fell to my knees from the bench where I'd been sitting and wrapped my arms around myself. I sobbed so loudly that my three cell-mates woke up.

"Shut up! It's light out," said one.

Another answered, "That's the new girl. She moaned all night. I could barely sleep a wink."

"Yeah," said the one who'd comforted me. "I was kind to you when you couldn't sleep. You actually snored like a buzzing bee."

I looked at the one who had just spoken. I was sur-prised—so surprised that I couldn't keep myself from gasping aloud. I had thought I'd see an ugly, repellent monster, yet I saw the pretty, pale face of a child. Misery and dirt were imprinted on her fresh face, and she had kind eyes and lovely little white teeth. Her bare chest revealed her slender, well-formed neck.

She sat on her rear, threw her messy, frizzy hair back, and looked at me on the bench, stunned. "Wait!" she said. "I thought you were sleeping next to me!"

Poor child. I didn't dare tell her why I'd gotten up. "I move around a lot," I told her. "I wanted to let you sleep and stretch myself out."

The dearie tilted her head, looked me in the face, and said, "That's not true. That's not why you moved. I dis-gusted you; I'm foul. It's my fault." She looked at me with an air of kindly reproach. "It's all the same. But it's better that you sleep with me rather than near Rose, who's in the corner. She has scabies."

I looked at Rose. She seemed fine. She was dressed like the sellers in the market, with a scarf on her head.

Mlle Rose was short and about fourteen. She got up in a fury, stomping across the mattresses. She went over to the raggedy girl and said threateningly, "You lie. I don't have scabies; those are spots of blood. If you say it again, I'll thrash you."

My neighbor didn't seem very afraid. She stood up and said, "If you beat me, I'll be annoyed because I'd have to touch you, but I won't leave a mark on you. I'm not the strongest, but I'll yell. They'll put you in the dungeon, and we'll be shut of you. You'll be able to make peace with your blood spatter." Then she laughed like a madwoman.

"It's true," said Rose. "Anyway, I don't want to dirty myself beating up a beggar." And she turned around, took a mattress, arranged it in a corner, then sat down.

The beggar took hers and carried it over to put it on the other. Rose got up without saying anything. Peace had been made.

The beggar said to the girl lying beside her, "Get up, then. The guard is coming. If the beds aren't put up and the blankets folded, you'll be punished."

The girl she was talking to pushed off the covers and extended her arms so I could see her face and dress. She must have been eight or nine; her skin was tanned. Her black hair was tangled. Two velour scarves were wrapped around her head, and she had brass earrings. She wore a black cotton velour jacket and a plaid skirt. Her booties, too big for her feet, were tied on with string.

"Come on, then," the beggar said, pushing the girl again. "You're going to get us in trouble."

"Ah!" said the one still in bed. "I dreamed that I was singing on the Champs-Élysées—I was busking. I got forty sous." She pressed into her hands and got up. I saw her holey stockings. She was short, even at her full height. She put her bed onto the others.

All the mattresses were in a pile that served as seating during the day. The singer set herself down next to Rose. The beggar came over to sit on the other end of my bench.

I moved a little nearer to her. I was about to speak when the lock was turned and we heard an unnecessarily harsh voice.

"Your beds are put up? So I can sweep?"

"Yes," said my neighbor.

The door opened, and a man carrying a bucket entered. The guard stood at the door and said, looking toward me, "Who bawled all night?"

"Shut up! Now you can't even cry in prison?" said the beggar. "Maybe you think it's fun, with you being so friendly and all. We can't even ask you the time."

"That doesn't stop you from coming back, beggar!" said the jailer, moving to let the man with the bucket pass.

"It's not my fault I keep coming back here."

The jailer didn't answer because he knew very well he couldn't deny it.

Once the room had been swept, they left. The beggar called after them, "Send us soup."

This attitude was amazing to me. You could get out of this prison and then end up coming back again. But how could that even happen?

I asked the girl next to me, "Why are you here?"

"Because I begged for money on the street."

"Why?" I think my question seemed odd to her, and she wanted to laugh at me. But I was so distraught that she didn't have the heart.

She said, "To eat, obviously."

"You don't have a father or mother?"

"Oh, I have a mother. My father was a roofer. He was killed on the job five years ago. There are five children, and I'm the oldest. Maman darns stockings when she can get the work. So me and my brother, one day there wasn't any bread in the house, and since we were hungry, we left without telling anyone, and we went out begging. That night, I had fifteen sous, my brother nine, and I'm pretty sure he'd made what I did, but he ate some cake. Maman fed our littlest sister. She was very tired from having to deprive herself for us. When we told her where we got the money, she wanted to be mad. I had bought bread, milk, and sugar for my little sister, but my mother began to weep and scold me! I did it again the next day. This was great fun, because I always made more than my brother. One day, I asked for money from a gentleman, who brought me here, and I stayed a week. Maman came looking for me. They saw that she was very malnourished, so they promised to help her and let me go. We were given one loaf of bread a week. That's not enough for six. I started begging again. I again saw the same man who'd brought me here, but he seemed not to see me. Another man did see me, and he arrested me two days ago. I was told this was my second chance, that they couldn't hold me here, and that they were sending me to detention. That's fine by me! I could learn to read and work there. Without that, I'd always be a beggar. And you," she said to me, "what have you done, then?"

"Me," I said, "I didn't do anything."

"Me too," said the singer, who'd joined the conversation. "I play guitar outside cafés. We were an ensemble: a hurdy-gurdy player, a woman who played harp, and a violinist. They kept all the money, and I worked for free. That didn't seem right, so I quit the group. Three days ago, I was arrested on the Champs-Élysées in front of a café. Two gentlemen had brought me up into their room to sing, and I was arrested for it." This girl was nine. She lied with incredible ease. She'd been on her own for two years. She had gotten out of detention to go to a hospital.

"Oh," said the one called Rose, "if they take you to detention, you won't get out! You know that I sell bouquets on the Champs-Élysées; you can't put one past me. Jules didn't see you that night, he waited until I had sold my flowers."

"Tell me about your friend Jules," said the singer. "He's the little thief who always ran after me to take my money. They arrested you in the same roundup as him. They won't arrange for your things to be brought to you. They brought you in with a cop on either side until your scabies heal because it's a blood disease. I saw her scratch."

Mlle Rose was not pleased with the direction of this conversation. She said no more.

We were brought bread. It was a round, dark loaf with a crusty dome. You could do all kinds of things with the insides, as if it were putty.

The commissary was opened, and they called out, "Vendor! Who wants to buy something?"

Rose asked for white bread and sausage. The singer got bread and paper for writing. The beggar looked at me as if to say, *You don't have any money, do you?* Then, leaving her seat, she went to dance around the provisions. The singer gave her half her bread.

"Come on," Rose said to her. "Cut a little from my sausage before I've touched it at all, horrible vixen. And stop saying I have scabies!"

The beggar took half and said to her, "Give me a little of your bread." She came back to my bench and handed me half of what she had. "We can share."

My first reaction was to push her hand away, but she seemed so upset at my refusal that I took half of her bread. I was so emotional! I wanted to hug her. I searched for something I could give her, but sadly I had nothing. Then an idea came to me: I got up and took off my colorful overskirt. I had made it from a woolen dress. It was very nice, and as my dress was lined, I could get by without it. I gave it to her. She was much shorter than me, so my skirt came far enough down to hide her bare feet. She jumped for joy.

"She's always first," said the singer.

Rose opened a little package and threw her a plaid scarf. "Here, wash it if you're afraid, and hide your neck."

The scarf was nice. The singer put it on immediately without thinking to say thank you.

I had arrived during the night, so the police came to take me for questioning.

"Goodbye," the beggar said. "Maybe you won't come back here if your mother's there."

I knew she wouldn't be. She probably wasn't even in Paris. In any case, there was no way she'd been told what had happened. Nevertheless, I hoped. You always hope when you want something so badly.

I was taken down the same stairs that I had come up during the night. I recognized the door at the bottom where I had entered and the vestibule where I had waited. There were two city policemen and three women, and I was placed near them.

"You're going to take six," said the warden.

"Yes," said the policeman.

I approached him and asked, "Is it me you're going to take? Where are you going to take me?"

He laughed without answering, so I addressed one of the women.

"To the doctor's," she answered tersely.

I looked at this woman and her two companions. One had tousled gray hair sticking out from under a poorly tied kerchief. She used tobacco and smelled of brandy. The other, who said that she liked being at the school gate more than here, had on a red-and-green dress and a hat covered with flowers. The one who'd answered me could have been thirty; she seemed nice enough. Her outfit was decent and elegant. I didn't see how she found herself with these women who horrified me.

Just then the guard left the room for the ground floor, where I had passed through some time before. Two other women followed. I recognized one of them as Thérèse, the woman who had been arrested with me. I was about to throw myself toward her when I saw her look away. I understood that I was not to speak to her here. I waited.

We were lined up—a guard in front, another behind—and we went out.

The entryway was full of people, men and women. They were waiting for someone they knew to come out. I can only tell you how I suffered to see this. The idea of passing through this room with the policemen, like criminals, and hearing them insult these women—hearing them insult me—almost made me die of shame. I hid my head in my hands, which drew more mockery in my direction. I heard, "Well, she's ugly, that one. She hides her face."

I sobbed. Thérèse said to me quietly, "Don't cry. Say

what I told you to M. Régnier, and he will take you to your mother's."

We crossed the courtyard and were on rue Jerusalem. There was a group of women accompanied by policemen who came out through an entryway. We waited until they were gone to go in ourselves. They had us go up two flights, then brought us into a room where there were already other women waiting. This room was bare: benches along four walls, and a window that overlooked a shady courtyard. Thérèse came to sit near me.

"All right, then," she said, "have a little courage. How was it up there? You didn't have any money. Wait, here are three francs. If you go back, you can't eat the house bread. If I'm let out—and I hope I am—I'll go to your house to ask for your mother or get her address wherever she is. If I'm unlucky enough to be sentenced to a month or two, and you get out after that, which isn't at all likely—I wouldn't be afraid," she said when she saw me blanch. "But there are formalities, and you can only be released to your parents. That can't take more than a week."

"A week!" I cried. "But I'll be dead in a week. If they take me back to the place I left, I'll kill myself."

"Be quiet; they can hear us. If you sob like that, we'll be separated. I won't be able to talk to you anymore."

Just then two names were called. I watched the mix of happy and sad, of tears and joy, of the ones who were going back inside and the ones who were laughing.

"I'm acquitted!"

"I'm out tonight!"

They took messages from the others who went back inside weeping.

"I'll be transferred tomorrow. I got two months."

I saw yet another pale, exhausted woman, who said to her friends, "I'm ill. I'm going to the hospital."

The old paupers watched it all without emotion, without repentance or pity. The youngest among them wept and asked God for forgiveness for their downfall and promised Him they would repent. I don't know if any of them kept their word, but surely right then they were sincere.

Peals of laughter answered their pleas. These oaths, these words were so cynical that the guard threatened to throw them in the dungeon if they continued. Two of these women were drunk and didn't seem like they wanted to sober up.

Thérèse was called. I stood and took her hand so I would be allowed to leave with her. She signaled with her head and shoulder to say, *I'm a prisoner myself; you can't come with me.* I fell back onto the bench, no longer hearing any of the muddled noise. The door opened again without my taking note. They said my name. They brought Thérèse back in and said, "The little one in front."

"Go," she said to me as she helped me up.

Leaving one prison for another can seem like a step toward freedom. I ran toward the door.

"Hey, sweetie, not so fast," the guard said, taking me by the arm. "Wait until we leave."

We were in an office that served as a waiting room. There was a ring from the room next door, and I was taken into another room where there were many crates and a large desk. A man sat behind it. I didn't dare take even a step toward him.

He said without raising his head, "Approach!" His voice made me tremble like a leaf. My teeth chattered so hard he heard and said, "Come on, don't be dumb.

Answer my questions. I don't have time to waste."

This was evident. He asked my name twice, but I couldn't answer. Seeing that I was not in any state to speak, he said more kindly, "Let's start again. You were arrested yesterday with a vulgar woman who gave you shelter in order to corrupt you. Did she give you any advice? What did you see at her place? Tell me the whole truth; it's the only way to earn your freedom."

I had the advantage in reflecting on this poor girl who had been compromised by her good heart. I answered in a firm voice that contrasted in every way with how I had felt when I came into this room.

He looked at me suspiciously. "Were you homeless when she found you? Why didn't you go home to your mother?" He looked at me as if he wanted to read the depths of my soul. It seemed that this test was trending in my favor, because he started again. "But, my poor child, if your mother isn't in Paris, I'm obligated to keep you here until she comes. Instead of writing by post, I'll send an officer."

He rang, and they came to get me. Thérèse was waiting impatiently for me.

"Good!" she said. "What happened?"

"I have to stay here to wait for my mother," I answered, distraught and not comprehending the full meaning of her question. But my distraction didn't last long. "Sorry," I said. "I forgot that your release is pending too. I hope that you're going to get out soon."

I went to sit at the back of the room, pressing my back against the wall. My poor head was so heavy that I could no longer hold it up.

Thérèse was called. I squeezed her hand. So many emotions overwhelmed me. I couldn't say a word.

She came back joyfully—she was going to get out. The very idea revived me. I looked at her with envy. She was free, and I was staying. What had I done? Why hadn't she left me where she'd found me? Another woman would have brought me somewhere so that I wouldn't end up in prison. I followed her so I could share my criticism.

She gave me time to cool off, then she said, "You shouldn't have said that. I meant well. I'm more angry about it than you."

She was right. I was being unfair. "I was wrong," I said, "but I'm so miserable! Will my mother believe me? This man has turned her head."

"Rest easy. I will see her."

They called Thérèse, and we went back to the station, where she would be released.

When we passed through the cursed door and I heard it close behind me, it was as if my heart was crushed by the hinges.

All the women took different paths. I alone went up the stairs.

They were waiting for me at the top. When they opened the door, my beggar stepped up to me, laughing.

"There you are. I was afraid you'd gotten out." This was rather friendly, but I kept my guard up. She had a lot of questions that I didn't answer. She stretched out and said, "You're so vain!"

I pulled myself together. "I'm not vain," I said, "but I have a lot on my mind. You're too young to understand."

She thought otherwise. "News came while you were downstairs. The singer left."

I looked toward her mattress and saw two children sleeping, or trying to sleep. "Do you know why they're here?"

"Non. I asked, but they didn't answer. The bigger one is mean."

The door opened, and they called for Céleste. I thought someone had come looking for me. I ran to the door. They handed me a package and a piece of paper. I read:

> *My dear Céleste,*
>
> *Don't make yourself sad. I'm going to see your mother. I'm sending you a nightgown, soap, a towel, and a scarf. I got out of jail, but I will not forget you. I regret being what I am. You'll have news from me before long.*
>
> *Thérèse.*

Night came. The mattresses were arrayed on the floor like cots. The beggar made a bed apart from the others and said to me, "That's for you, over there."

The two new girls began to fight. They were sisters.

"It's your fault," said one. "I said to be careful, but you always have to mess around."

"It's not my fault," said the younger. "The lady twisted the straps of her bag around the chair rung twice. I thought I could still get it, but the chair moved, and the old lady woke up. I brought the bag to you. She let me take it, and then she had us arrested. Is that my fault?"

"Be sure you say you just picked the bag up off the ground. If you say anything else, you'll be in trouble."

"But if the lady said that I brought it to her—"

"You said that it wasn't true. And if you say that it's me who told you to steal, you'll have to deal with me when we get out of here." And with that, she stepped over her sister.

The little one shrank back, almost between my legs. I

had her move behind me and said to her sister, who was a petite brunette with round, dark eyes and a turned-up nose, "Leave the little one alone. Are you going to beat her now? She's going to tell the truth. It's your fault first, then hers. You're older, and you told her to do wrong."

She began to hurl insults at me and wanted to get around behind me. I was never tough, but I was always strong. With one shove, I sent her rolling across the room. Luckily for her, the mattresses were out. She charged at me, furious, saying that she'd cut me with a knife—in a genuine rage.

"Try it," said my beggar. "I'll yell and tell them you wanted to fight us."

This threat scared her. She turned to her sister and held up her fist. "You'll pay for these bitches!"

"I know," said the little one. "You want to bust me up, but I won't come near you." She tucked herself into my bed.

❧

I went six days and six nights without any news, without a single word. I'd been drained of all my courage. There was nothing anyone could say to make me feel better. I had definitely been abandoned. I was going to go to prison.

The next day, they came for all four of us. They told us to take all our things, that we were leaving the jail. We went down to the vestibule, where we were called. There were eleven of us waiting.

"Next stop, prison," said the guard, and all four of us were taken outside.

I saw a large carriage, like a bus but with bars all

around. I shrank back and cried, "I can't go in that."

Someone pulled on my dress. It was Thérèse, who had watched me exit from the shadowy stairway.

"Have you seen my mother?" I asked.

"Non, she hasn't returned. I can't write to you; you can't receive letters in prison. Be patient; I won't forget you. That man at your mother's house knows where you are. I told him. He doesn't want to give me your mother's address, but I'm watching for her return." Then the women left; she fled.

"Why'd you let the prisoners talk?" said the jailer to the policeman.

"Aren't they prisoners of the state?"

"Are you kidding? I'd rather have conspirators than these women. They're feisty."

"Not always," said the guard as he climbed up into the carriage.

"Bah, that's the stuff they're made of. Let's go, into the carriage." And he went past me to climb up.

I was terrified to find myself inside this iron cage. I wanted to throw myself to the ground. "I don't want to stay in here!" I thrashed about between the other five or six women.

"If you aren't quiet, I'm going to toss you in the dungeon," said the guard.

"Monsieur," I yelled louder, "have pity on me! Keep me here one more day. My mother will come tomorrow. I didn't steal! I'm begging you, let me out!" I fell on my knees, and I held my arms out to him.

He pushed the door and said, "Instead of going to detention, we should be headed for the asylum at Charenton."

The carriage began to move. I lost all hope. I let

myself roll under the others' feet. I felt someone pick me up and put me on a seat. I opened my eyes, my mind blank, and I began to weep.

"Go ahead and cry," said my little Rosalie (that's what the beggar was called). "It'll make you feel better."

I had spent days combing her hair, washing her. She was kind and good. I still couldn't see inside the carriage. Her mere presence made me feel better, and I hugged her so tightly I could have suffocated her.

The carriage stopped. We heard someone call out, "Gate, please!"

We entered the Saint-Lazare prison.

7.

DENISE

OUR CARRIAGE PAUSED. THE GATE opened, and we went in under an archway. The sound of the wheels rolling along was foreboding. My breath left me. I could not possibly have been any more depressed. The doors closed behind me.

I heard a voice cry out, "Here's the prisoner transport; come see the new girls. Are there a lot?"

Another voice, surely that of another driver, said, "That's all of 'em. I'm done."

They had us get out. A man stepped in front of us, and a sheet of paper was handed to him. "Ah," he said, "from corrections. Where are the thieves?"

The idea that I could be confused with a thief made me look toward the two sisters as if I wanted to point them out.

"Let's go," said the man. "Follow me."

We went through the barred gates, down the hallways, across the courtyards, and into a large room, where they left us. There was a double grille in the middle of the room, with two feet between each set of bars. This was a parlor where you could chat while keeping your distance.

The women who'd been convicted didn't yet know how long they'd be there. Their anxiety had a very different character. One of them said, "Maybe I only got a month! I fought with my husband at a wine merchant's. A police sergeant found us there. It was my fault."

"I'm only afraid of one thing myself," murmured an old lady who was seated on a bench, "that they won't give me a long enough sentence. It's only been a week since I got out, but I don't have any other shelter. I'm only happy at Saint-Lazare."

Despite myself, I shivered at the idea that you could like a prison. I asked a woman next to me, "Do you know, madame, when they send you to prison, how much time you'll get?"

"That depends on your age. They can keep you until you're twenty-one."

"Six years!" I cried. "You're just saying that to scare me. They can't have the right to keep me againts my will for six years?"

I turned to a girl from the City, one of those vile women without a heart, without a soul, who insult the unfortunate and never help the downtrodden, who swear every chance they get, who make a virtue of their vices. These women say to one another: "I drank a bottle of brandy! I have stabbed—and have been stabbed—however many times! I have a famous thief for a lover!" Anyone who can brag like this is admired by the others. These women wear a scarf over their ears; it's a sign of belonging. They are the terror of inspectors because when they are taken in, they fight back. Often there are dangerous brawls between them and the police.

I addressed myself to one of those creatures. She was only too glad to make my life even worse. "All the little tramps," she said loudly, "they've fucked us over. It wouldn't bother me if they were put in a cage. You're so sure of your situation, go on! You won't be joking soon enough! When I found out about them myself, I busted them."

I began to cry; she began to sing:

There is no pleasure without pain

Tra la la

"Don't cry," said another. "It only makes the punishment twice as bad."

Luckily they called for us, because I was about to talk back. That would have made a worse mess of things.

❧

Night came. The man who came in lifted his lamp to see us and recognized many of us. "There are the season ticket holders!"

They led us into an office where one name was called after another.

"La Huche!"

The City woman who'd been so mean to me stepped forward, head held high, fist on her hip.

The man read from a sheet of paper: "La Huche, for fighting in public, three months."

She ran at the warden, fists balled, and pummeled him. The guards kicked her out as she frothed. For several seconds, the most horrible oaths could be heard.

"A week in the dungeon," said the warden, writing at the bottom of the paper, still pale from the shock.

A paper was read for each of us. Then it was the two sisters' turn.

"The Thion girls! For stealing the purse of a lady on the Champs-Élysées, three years in prison."

"Send them to children's court."

It was only me and the beggar left. I waited; I hoped that they'd given me a sentence.

"Which of you two is Céleste?"

"Me, monsieur," I said, stepping into the light.

"You've never been here before?"

"Non, monsieur."

"You've never been arrested?"

"Non, monsieur."

"Take these two rebels," he said, directing us toward the guard. "You'll register the girl Céleste." Then he added as if speaking to himself, "It's no use. If she's only gone half bad now, she'll be entirely bad after being among all these characters."

We turned down a few corridors to find ourselves in an enormous hallway. There were small, numbered doors all along the walls on both sides. We were told to stop once we got halfway down. Two doors were open, and each of us was made to enter a cell.

I walked forward, groping. I found an iron bed, so I sat down and ended up falling asleep still dressed.

꧁꧂

The day began at first light, when I was awakened by someone who spoke in a whisper at the foot of my bed.

Each cell had a large window with bars and grates where panes of glass should be. This window looked out onto the corridor, where someone was chatting.

"You knew very well that it's forbidden to speak to noncompliant," the voice said. "If you want to spend another month here, be my guest."

Then profound silence. I couldn't sleep any longer.

A bell rang, my door opened, and a woman came in carrying clothing. She told me to undress and gave me the uniform blouse. Across the front was written Prison Saint-Lazare. I put my hand underneath it to keep the fabric from touching my skin. It seemed as if the words would be imprinted on my body.

"Hold out your arms so I can try this dress on you."

She handed me a kind of sack in gray homespun, a blue apron with a thousand stains, a black wool hat in three pieces with no lace, and a cotton scarf with flowers. Not having clogs for my feet, she let me keep my slippers.

I saw many heads dressed like mine crowd in the doorway to see me. It's always like this when a new person arrives.

One, stronger than the others, pushed on my door and said, "You can leave; the bell rang. If you want, I can take you to the refectory."

"Line up in order by rank!"

We all lined up, two by two. They put me at the end with a young girl my size. We went up to what they called the refectory. There were three very long tables with wood benches on either side. A group prayer was said, then we were given soup. Everyone finished at the same time.

We spent time in a class arranged so that you could take lessons in writing, vocal music, and math. The class lasted two hours. They next led us into a workshop, and each girl took her place. We embroidered crepe de chine.

Between two windows was an elevated desk where Mlle Benard sat. She was a pleasant enough woman of about thirty. She showed us our seats, and she said some welcoming words to me. I quickly thought of her as a friend. She was too sweet, too kind for the devils she had chosen to manage.

At noon we had a second meal, then we went down for recreation in an enclosed area that had no trees or flowers. The walls all around were fifty feet high. We played all kinds of games. The oldest went off two by two and spoke very little to the youngest. The older girls loved each other to the point of being jealous of any friendship with others.

There was one girl named Denise who from the first day attached herself to me. She gave me little presents, maybe a needle, maybe a feather. She was not stingy with compliments. One day her girlfriend became so jealous of me that she made a scene. Mlle Benard told me not to speak to Denise anymore.

So Denise wrote to me. One of her letters was discovered, and she was put in solitary confinement. When she got out after a week, she came to where I was working, hugged me, and said, "They can put me in solitary, in the dungeon, for the rest of my life. That won't stop me from loving you always."

Mlle Benard scolded me for allowing myself to be embraced. I answered that I couldn't help Denise's feelings of friendship toward me.

Denise was a real tomboy. Her face was straightforward, strong; nothing scared her. When she was punished, she sang. She was unbreakable. Since they had forbidden her from speaking to me, she sent me word of meeting places. She always had something to tell me. We developed an affectionate connection. Instead of avoiding occasions to see her, I looked for them. When she spoke to others, it was now my turn to sulk.

She sent me charming drawings that she made herself with the colorful silk braids that we used to embroider shawls, or white paper flowers and birds. The attendant didn't see any of this.

When the others played in the evening after work, I went to sit under a window—not to look out onto the street; that wasn't possible, because there was an awning above the lower window—but to hear the passing carriages and the calls of the merchants. The Normans who sold lettuce in baskets seemed so lucky to be free! I would have given years of my life to be free for one day.

Denise came up and said to me, "Ingrate! You want to get out! To leave me and do whatever you want while I stay here." She began to sob.

"It's true, I do want to leave. I'll try to help get you out."

"There's nothing to be done for me. I still have six more months. I want to be registered as a prostitute. You have to be sixteen. If your people don't come for you, you can do the same. I know good houses where they give you a lot of money." She told me the address of the one where she was planning to go.

I didn't take much notice…then.

She repeated it twenty times. "You'll come see me, right?" She was so insistent that I promised.

But I still told her to give up on her idea. That life was the most miserable in the world. I was thinking of Thérèse.

"That's not right," she said. "You've only seen the low-class women, the ugly or drunk ones. But I know plenty myself who've made a small fortune, who have beautiful apartments, jewelry, carriages, who only deal with the highest-class clients. If I were as pretty as you, I would quickly get business. Meanwhile, you'll be well on your way to marrying a laborer who beats you, maybe, or makes you work to support the both of you. And then you'll end up back here. You'll do great. They'll know you and shame you."

"I don't believe that. I'm not made for a life of crime."

She began to laugh and said, "How do you know that?"

I had no answer.

She started up again. "All the same, whatever you do, come see me when we're both out. I don't want to be like these brazen women who go around with their noses in the air to show the effect they have on a thousand people, to be known in all of Paris. I'll stay in a house, I'll put money aside, then after a while I'll live however I want. You can come with me."

It was time to go inside for the night. We went quietly.

Everything Denise had told me danced in my head all night. I saw myself as rich, covered in jewels and lace. I looked in my little piece of mirror. I really was pretty, though wearing this uniform did not help.

Then, all of a sudden, I was ashamed of thinking about everything that I was going to have.

❧

On Sunday, we went to mass in our uniforms. All sections of Saint-Lazare were there, but kept apart with the utmost precaution.

The chapel was set up like the Chantereine theater. On either side of the altar a set of stairs led to a gallery behind a lattice. On one side were the young thieves, who were called the petite persecuted. On the other side, where I was, sat the noncompliant. There was a definite distinction between the doomed and the unruly. They had the deepest scorn for one another.

Surveillance was extreme. The columns of girls could only go out one after the other so that they couldn't come into contact. All communication was severely punished.

The lower level was also designed like a theater with dividers, like the stalls for the orchestra and audience.

The girls from corrections always entered first and exited last. Behind me, Denise gave me all the details as we walked in.

"Hey, see those entering over there and sitting in the front? Those are the adulterers and the battered women. Those on the other side are waiting for a hearing. They've been here for six months. They might be acquitted, but they're here for at least six months."

A third column of women entered and was placed behind the first two. "Look out for those women," Denise said, "and be on your guard if you meet them later on. They're thieves. When they receive short sentences, they keep them here."

All of the women entered quietly and with appropriate contemplation, but soon we heard a ruckus. A group of women had made their way to the back, in the area that I compared to the audience's seats in a theater. They were shoving one another. They had tried to sit in the first pews, maybe to better hear the crowd, but with such rudeness that the guards had to intervene. It was very curious to see. Everyone wore almost exactly the same uniform as we did.

Each condemned woman came down the stairs to the workshops. In those days they had to make boxes of matches. They were very good workers, and since they were forced to do it, they had a great pile of money when they got out. It was a mix from which you couldn't steal an idea.

People who I would later meet as elegant and proud women I saw here in this sad and shameful uniform. There were old women disfigured by scars and sickness; there were very young and pretty women. Almost all of these lost souls had a certain flair. Some had a lace cap under their uniform hat; others had white camisoles and silk scarves.

The most elegant belonged to brothels. The mistresses of these houses needed them and so sent them linens, money, and provisions every week. People said, "So-and-so got an entire basket!" They were the aristocracy of the place. They also had an old woman with no family in their section of the prison who served them and did their work. There were some who had money; men they had attended to when they were on the outside sent them plenty. For the most part they were generous, and they paid for everyone. They were called les Panuches. During the service, all these women looked around, chatted, and passed little notes to women from the infirmary, to the thieves, to the unsentenced. They signaled to the corrections officers and were taken to them. While the attendants heard mass, all these little games went on. They blew kisses to say goodbye! Sunday was really a party.

Denise had been in corrections for three years. She had a friend who had aged into the women's quarters and so was in one of the other columns of women that came in. Denise leaned over and put two fingers through the grate. She wanted to point out the Blonde, as she called her, to me.

"Okay, do you see the bench at the rear, there's a woman who has a kerchief with large checks, next to the one-eyed woman? This woman with her head lowered and blonde hair, and a blue-and-white scarf around her neck?"

"Yes, but I can't see her face."

Denise moved closer to the grate. "She's writing on her lap. There, she lifted her head. What do you think of her?"

I watched carefully before answering. She was a girl of probably eighteen or twenty. Her hair was so beauti-ful that I looked above her head to see if there wasn't a sunbeam giving her this shining, golden color. Her eyes were large and of a gentle blue; their wide, sweet expres-sion said she had a weak character. Her forehead was framed by two curls. The style looked good on her; she knew it and defied the rules by curling it every day. Her face was long, as was her nose, though it was a little flat on the end. Her bottom lip stuck out farther than the top; her mouth was large, and she had crooked teeth, but they were white. She had ugly parts, but nevertheless her white skin, her beautiful eyes, and her hair, which fell on either side of her blunt chin, made her an attractive woman. She seemed about four and a half feet tall; her shoulders were broad and a little high.

I told Denise, who was waiting, a tiny bit of my impression. "It's a funny face. The lower half is awful, common; the top half is handsome. What's she like? She seems nice."

"She is," Denise said, "but she has a personality like her face. That is to say, she's both. She is whimsical, insouciant. You can say or do rotten things to her, and it won't bother her. Then the next day, without anyone saying anything, she loses her temper. You might think she's a little insane. She was raised well. She ran away from her parents' house because of her stepmother. That's when she entered a house."

I turned my head and saw, near the grate by me, a little girl of twelve or thirteen who was making intense efforts to be seen by those below. "Look how this little one squirms about."

"It's to try to get her mother, who is one of the unsentenced, to see her. Do you see that large woman who turns her head toward our side of the room? That's her mother. She pimped out her daughter, so she's going to get at least three years. The child did what she could to defend her mother, but the other daughter told them that her mother had sold this older girl two years before, turned her in, and charged her with extortion because her mother had made her take the stage for money."

The woman horrified me. I looked away.

At the other end of the bench where the unsentenced sat there was a dark, delicate little girl who looked as if she were having a hard time. I noted her to Denise.

"That's the woman just out of the maternity ward, that is! She made a huge fuss on her way in. She was married to a brave man who adored her. He gave her everything she wanted, and as he had a very successful business, there was nothing too beautiful for his wife. But she was very brusque, very severe with everyone else.

She was not at all liked. Her husband was away for a year. When he came back, a kind neighbor told him he had been a father for a week. It seems that this news did not make him nearly as happy as you might think, because he came back that night with the police. He had his wife arrested, as well as his assistant, who was supposed to look after her. The husband, who had been a sheep, turned into a wolf."

"Poor woman!" I said as I looked at her. "She should be pitied."

"You find her pitiable?" said Denise in astonishment. "I don't pity her. It's her fault. People weren't robbed. If she didn't like this man, she shouldn't have married him. If you can say yes, you can also say no. When I get out of here, if someone wants to marry me, I'll refuse because I want to be free. Another—a woman like her, for example—could get married and be free anyway.

"Wait—look at the second woman in the sixth row; that's a woman to pity! You can see that she's pretty. She's from Bordeaux. A handsome enough man proposed to her, and she married him, believing that he loved her. Not at all. He stuck her in a shop where her good looks drew people in. He ended up telling her what he wanted from her, then he sold her to the highest bidder and beat her like a rug when she refused. The police got involved, and they arrested the both of them. He gave his consent to divorce in order to free her to be registered. I would have strangled him myself, but I guess she adored him. I think she's scared."

"I don't pity her. That's a woman without heart, without character. That's a machine. Who told you all that?"

"The chambermaid who works the corridor. She's my friend."

The mass ended, and everyone went out in the order they had come in. We went downstairs. At the last step, Denise bent down and picked up something that she tucked into her scarf.

As we entered the garden, she led me to a corner and pulled out a piece of paper folded up very small.

"She likes me more than you do," she said. "It's been more than two years since she got out. She didn't forget me." Then she read:

> *My dear, the time is coming when you are going to take flight. If I were to do it again, I wouldn't. I had no luck; it's my third stint. I passed the night in a hotel in the Latin Quarter. I was taken in by the patrol, and here I am for a month. I'm depressed; it's far from what I expected for myself. If you don't receive my note, it's not my fault. I'm worried I misunderstood your signal. I think of you often. I am going to hate prison.*
>
> *Marie la Blonde.*

"You see that you were wrong yesterday when you said that women could possibly be happy in this life," I said.

"But I say it again," answered Denise as she refolded the letter. "Marie doesn't have any willpower. She's infatuated with a student who goes to see her. She doesn't go out at all; he takes her to his house."

❧

At that time, there were about forty of us in prison. It was a true republic—we argued and fought endlessly.

One day, two of the worst inmates quarreled in the

shop. Then Mlle Benard came in.

"Can it," said one of them. "We'll meet again in the garden."

I thought this meeting would be forgotten. Not at all. They went to a corner and beat each other, kicking and punching.

There was incredible perversity and astonishing audacity among the inmates. One girl of twelve took flight over the walls, which were between seventy and eighty feet high. Another escaped via the laundry.

At last, just as all who are isolated become overl amorous, these children, these women, found the smallest reasons to chat and write to one another. What wreaked the most havoc were the liaisons between the girls of twelve and fifteen years old and women of thirty or forty. They managed to get around the most diligent surveillance.

Every letter that came in or out was read and marked. Despite all the precautions, the hiring women found ways to practice their infamous trade. These so-called hiring women would go find a pretty girl and give her the address of the disreputable houses that they represented, singing their praises. They put ideas into the heads of the poor children, who they pulled out of schools or from the streets and into sleazy hovels where, if they were sickly, they died young. What is more horrible is the perversity of corruption in this hellish place. It's not rare to hear of children ten years old saying they want to be prostitutes when they're older.

The visitor's room was on the ground floor, corrections on the third. There was a pipe in the wall that came up from below. When it rang, it was a signal to press your ear against the trumpet. They'd ask to speak to someone;

everyone raised their heads, everyone hoped. Whoever was called ran out like a madwoman, and the others were disappointed. Then, when she came back up with food, all the others surrounded her. She had seen someone from the outside; it was as if she brought news from another world.

I'd been there a month without anyone giving me a sign of life. That's what makes it hard. When you're sentenced, you count each hour, each minute, as you await deliverance. When a friend writes you, you know that someone is thinking of you. But nothing! Nothing! So I had moments of rage when, carried away by my emotions, I planned my revenge to make everything worse for everyone. These moments of exasperation didn't last long, but they curdled my heart.

We had with us a girl named Augustine who was near my age. This girl was inexhaustibly happy; when I was down, Denise would go looking for her. I can only compare her to a monkey. One day she announced that her father had decided to get her out of prison.

"I persuaded him that I would get even worse than I was if I stayed here, and he believed me," she said with a burst of laughter. "Poor, good-natured Father, I'm going to lose him at the end of the street."

I told her that was awful.

"Thank you," she said. "He promised that if I conducted myself badly, he would not only use his lash on me, but some kind of punishment that is not at all pleasant. In order to get out, I said that I agreed, but I know how he acts. I'd rather give myself some space."

That night, Augustine found me in the hall and said in a serious voice, "I have something to ask you."

I thought she was going to wish me well. I followed

her into a corner, but I was a little suspicious.

She stopped me, checked to see if anyone was listening, and said, "I'm leaving tomorrow. I don't have any clothes. We're the same size; would you lend me yours? I'll send them back to you in two days. I'm going to go to a house, and they'll give me clothes. I'll quickly bring back what you lend me. Only don't tell anyone, because it's against the rules."

I told her that this was all I had, that if I loaned it to her, she'd have to get it back to me as soon as possible.

She made many promises. I believed she was sincere and agreed.

She left.

Some days later, since she hadn't sent me anything, I shared some of my worry with Denise.

"Dummy! Why didn't you say anything? This will be funny when it's time for you get out."

"The uniform comes with a bag to bury me in. I'm never leaving here."

"There you go with your dark thoughts. Come on, that's the bell for recreation. Come down."

I followed her.

In our enclosure, there was a door that everyone was curious about. You had to go up two stairs to enter it. We never saw it open. We always tried to see, through a window or a hole, what happened inside. Since we never found anything out, each of us had our own idea. There were interns who worked there, but they were not allowed to enter from our side. They had to enter and exit by another door that gave onto the hospital corridor. I was mostly ignorant of what went on behind this myste-rious door, but I wasn't any less intrigued than the others.

This particular day, it seemed that the key to the

other door had been misplaced. The interns had been coming in using the little door. It had been left ajar.

I had come down with Denise, who left me to go speak to someone else. When I passed near the door, I went up the two stairs and pushed gently. It opened. I leaned forward. Suddenly I stood up straight, as if a coiled spring inside me had been released. What I saw was frightening. I stiffened against the stone doorframe and attached myself to it. I saw, stretched out on a marble table, a young girl with her throat and chest open. She was not disfigured, but her eyes were half open. The light coming through the door shined on her face. I thought she was moving. I stared at her so hard my vision clouded over. I placed my hands on the wall behind me; I stood with my neck tensed, my mouth open. It was the infirmary's dissection theater.

"What are you doing?" said Denise as she approached.

I made a heroic effort to free myself from the wall, where I seemed to be embedded, and threw myself into her arms.

She led me down the stairs and asked, "Are you crazy? If this is how you distract yourself from dark thoughts, you chose well!"

I wanted to forget what I had seen. It was too much for me. *What a fate!* I said to myself. *So young! So pretty! Without a parent, without a friend, to be there to gather your remains. My God, is it you who created our burden?*

I passed an awful night. One of us had died. I was so upset that I changed my perspective.

❧

One day, I got up in a good mood, almost happy. I said

to my friend, "I don't know what's come over me. I had good dreams."

"Are you superstitious?" Denise laughed.

"No more than most people. My dreams rarely steer me wrong."

"Let's see. Tell me one. You dreamed that Saint-Lazare was overrun in an attack and you were given the key to the grounds."

I didn't say anything. I went to sit at my work. Each time the door opened, my heart raced. The hour rang out at the same time as the bell for the visiting room. The woman who listened for the name to be called hadn't heard it.

"It's me, right?" I exclaimed.

She turned back and said loudly, "Céleste, to the visiting room."

Instead of running as the others did, I stayed in my chair, so shaky that I couldn't get up.

"Take yourself down," said Mlle Benard. She never went down there.

Denise offered to come with me, and without waiting for an answer, she led me toward the stairway. I stopped on the second floor, my legs no longer obeying.

"What are you going to say to your mother?" she asked, stopping alongside me.

"I'm going to tell her everything that's happened."

"Well, yes, but as you said, she loves this man. Don't tell her without knowing if she ever saw anything. He'll have told her his side of the story. They could have forgotten you here."

We were at the bottom of the stairs. A warden made me go in, saying that my companion could wait at the door.

My mother was seated in a chair on the far side of the large room decorated with oak benches. The tiles where white, and there was a crucifix on the wall.

I lowered my head and waited. I had long ago lost the habit of hugging my mother. She didn't step toward me; I didn't dare approach.

"Whore!" she said at last. "You have no shame in making me come here."

I raised my head. The tone she used stunned me. I was so sure that it was me who had the right to blame her! At first I didn't know how to respond. Then, feeling the blood boil in my heart, I said, "I hope, my dear mother, that you know what drove me here and that you didn't just come to yell at me. You thought enough about me to come here. You probably have some grand idea of saving me. Yet here you are, and I'm not seeing that grand idea yet."

"This place hasn't changed your attitude any," she said. "It's only been three days since I found out you were here. That's how long it took me to get permission to come."

"Who receives your letters, then?"

"No one."

"They wrote to you five times."

"That's not true."

"How long have you been back in Paris?"

"A month."

"What were you told when you came home? You must have noticed I wasn't there."

"I was told the truth."

"And what is this truth?"

"That you had left to go along with a prostitute, and that you had been saved from that house."

"And who told you that?"

She didn't answer.

"How did you know that I was here?"

"Three days ago, a woman stopped me in the street, the one who had taken you. She told me where you were, making up I don't know what kind of story, telling me that she had come to our house twenty times, that she wasn't allowed to come up, that she'd been told I wasn't coming back to Paris."

"Did you ask the wine merchant if it was true?"

"No, why would he bother to guard my door?"

I hesitated a little, then said, "How is M. Vincent?"

"Fine," she said. "He came along. He's waiting for me outside."

I looked at the door. I thought of what Denise had said on the way down. It was as if I could see her laughing on the other side of the wall.

"Did you send a petition to the prefect to get me out of here?"

"I haven't had time yet. Vincent will do it tomorrow."

"No," I said, "have it written by someone else, and above all bring it yourself."

"Why?"

"I'll tell you later." I'd been in the visiting room with my mother for an hour. That's how long we got for a visit. "Don't forget to write. When will you come again?"

"In a few days. I'll write tomorrow."

She embraced me so coldly that as I ran up the stairs, I began to sob.

I said to Denise, "You were right; all is lost. I'm never leaving here. Poor Thérèse! I accused her of forgetting. *He* kept her from seeing my mother, and he kept the letters. This man will make me awful, hateful. I will get my revenge someday."

135

Time passed slowly. I planned a thousand things to say to my mother.

If I tell her everything, I thought, *and she believes me, great. But if she doesn't believe me, she'll leave me here. I must be patient. I'll tell Maman everything in front of him. He wouldn't dare contradict me.*

A week went by. My mother returned. She told me she had done as I asked and that in two or three days, I would be released.

On the third day, they came to my cell and told me to get dressed, that I'd be getting out in two hours.

"But I don't have any clothes," I cried. I hadn't been given my things. I'd forgotten to tell my mother. Did I have time to send someone out to look for clothes?

"No," said the guard, "not from here, but from the jail where you'll stay until tomorrow. They'll give you your things from prison; they'll be sent to you in a parcel."

I was in the cell with Denise. She started to cry so hard that my joy left me. I held her, I made all the promises I could. She dissolved into tears.

"I promise that I'll see you no matter where you go."

I spent my last two hours sitting on her bed. I hugged her one last time, and I left. I could still hear her sobbing from the end of the corridor.

I left as I had come, in the same carriage; only my uniform had changed. But I still didn't know the awful impression that the stint in prison would leave on me, the influence that these several months would have on my pathetic future.

When we arrived at the police station, they took me up to the room I'd been in before. There was a crowd: seven people were in this small space. I stayed there three days without sleeping and almost without eating.

The fourth day, M. Régnier asked for me. "My child, I wrote to you mother to come fetch you. Why didn't she come? And why are you in a prison uniform?"

"Monsieur, this is all I have."

"They forgot to send your clothes. Are you ill? You're very pale."

"Oh, Monsieur, if you knew where they'd put me. One of top of another. I was with a band of beggars from Alsace. I haven't eaten since I got here; it was disgusting."

"Let's go. I'm going to take you to the pistole." He drew two francs from his purse and gave them to me. "Here, you can eat with that." And he looked at me with such pity and shame that I will never forget it.

The goodness and humanity of M. Régnier didn't blind him to the grudges of those who dealt with him. At Saint-Lazare, they had a song about how much they hated him. Many times I heard him receive death threats. Only once did M. Régnier fall victim to his temper with one of those beings for whom the whole idea of discipline was unthinkable and who instinctively hated all those who were charged with maintaining order in society. At this time, women who'd been arrested were brought to M. Régnier's office, where he announced the sentences they'd received. One woman, who I tried to portray when I arrived at corrections, threw an enormous marble paperweight at this head. Luckily, it missed. The routine changed after that. The convicted are now taken to Saint-Lazare before they learn the length of their detention.

I don't know, from what I saw, if M. Régnier had ever pronounced a single unjust sentence in his life. Nevertheless, the women who hated him but couldn't let it loose in his presence plotted in the depths of their ulcerous hearts. I heard, not from one woman but from a hundred, "If there's a revolution, we're taking Régnier. If there's a riot, our men will burn Sainte-Lazare!"

Poor M. Régnier! So good to me and so many others. I often feared for his life.

On his orders, I was taken to the pistole. This was a room four feet square with a barred window, a strap bed, and a small table. All prisoners had the right, by paying one franc a day, to go to the pistole. Most preferred the common rooms; they were less desolate than this little room.

The rest of that day and that night were like a century.

At eleven a.m., I was called. I went into M. Régnier's office. My mother was there.

"You're about to leave, my child. Your mother has promised to watch over you. Listen to me: don't fall in with any of these women that you could meet, because if you come back here, you'll find me a strict judge. I'd send you to the convent of Saint-Michel until you turned twenty-one. They shave your head when you enter; your hair would have time to regrow before you got out."

I promised from the bottom of my heart to be wise. He said that if I ever came back, he would lock me up for the rest of my days.

I had to wait another hour for my things to be found.

At last the door opened. I was free!

8.

THE FALL

THE AIR WAS FILLED WITH fragrance. I breathed it in like an intoxicating flower that made me numb and circulated a new and unknown sense of well-being through my veins. "Free!" I cried, and I ran all the way to the docks without even looking around. I stopped at the wall by the river's edge to watch the water flow by. My thoughts were running along with it.

I was pulled out of my revery by my mother, who came to join me. As she tugged on my arm, she said, "Where are you going? This isn't the way home!"

"Sorry, my good mother," I said as I kissed her again and again. "Sorry! I must seem like a nut, oui? But I'm so happy! It's so nice to be free! Look at the river! How independent it is! It's all so lovely. I never noticed. It's true that you must have something taken from you before you know what it's worth. I love you, my wonderful mother!"

And I hugged her to annoy her.

"Calm down, you're wrinkling my dress. I'm glad you hold your freedom so dear. You won't mess up again."

I wasn't paying attention. "Oui, Maman," I said.

"We're going home. You'll work with me."

"Oui, Maman."

"Don't be trouble for poor Vincent."

That pulled me from my thoughts. I made her repeat it.

"You have to live in peace with him, for my sake," she said.

"How is that for your sake? Are you hoping to keep him around?"

This time it was she who stopped and looked at me in astonishment.

"So it's true," I said. "You only know what he's told you! I'm going to tell you the truth."

During my narrative, she reddened, then went white, then wept. I hurt her greatly. She had no response.

We arrived at the house. Vincent was at the window where I'd cut myself. My mother stomped up the stairs while my legs buckled. The sight of this house brought back everything, and the air suffocated me.

At last, I resolved to go upstairs fearlessly. *What am I afraid of?* I said to myself. *My mother is there. I'm going into her house. He cannot keep me out.*

I went in and looked Vincent in the face. I believe the sight of me bothered him, but not a muscle of his face moved.

My mother had the same idea as me. She stood next to me and said, "Go on, repeat in front of him what you told me on the way here."

I changed color and lost my bearings. I saw my

mother's face light up with a hope that gave me a bad fright. She doubted me. I couldn't believe it.

I moved forward, head high, gaze steady. Vincent gave no sign of emotion. His calmness was exasperating.

"Have you become mute?" I said to him. "Say why I left here. Say what happened! Fine. Then I will repeat everything that I told my mother."

When I was done, my mother said, "Answer her." This was as good as if she had said, "Say she's lying, and I'll believe you."

Vincent sensed his advantage. He was no longer stoic. "I was waiting until she was finished. I don't have any great speech to give. You know your daughter detests me. I knew her as a child, and thanks to you, I love her very much She came home very upset; I had to console her. I don't know what she expected. She ran away. She made up this story to get rid of me."

I became livid! I looked at my mother. Her face was calm. I clenched my teeth, and I felt my heart was too small to contain my anger and hate.

My mother was apparently scared of me in this state, because she asked him to leave us alone. He took his hat and went past me. His lips started to curl into a smile, which infuriated me.

"You believe him over me, don't you? He's laughing at me. He's so sure that you like him better, that he's everything in this house. Fine! He can have it. I certainly can't live here anymore. You've obviously decided to keep him. I'll leave."

My mother placed herself in front of the door and took me in her arms. "Come on, Céleste. Listen to me."

"Not if you can't promise to kick that man out."

"Fine, I'll leave him, but listen to me. He's going to

inherit a thousand francs. He's promised them to me to get me on my feet. Be patient for a while. I'll pretend to believe him. Just wait. When we move, I'll break up with him, and you and I, we'll stay together."

I was out of energy. Insomnia and emotion had drained me. I had dreamed of this scene, I had waited for something violent and decisive. I had told myself, *My mother has to choose between him and me.*

One minute would decide my fate. I had no sense of how this would turn out in the long run. The prolonged letdown took me by surprise and paralyzed my willpower. These calculating plans that my mother laid before me to postpone our leaving numbed my heart. I didn't understand this feeling then, what we call love having power over the soul of a woman her age; my mother was forty-seven then. I didn't cede ground, but I ceased to fight. That was all my mother wanted.

She dropped her stern mask, which in the depths of her heart she knew I didn't deserve to see on her face. She embraced me more enthusiastically than she had in a long time. I returned her embrace halfheartedly, but I returned it.

<hr>

I went to bed before Vincent came in, and I got up when he'd gone out. I avoided all occasions when I might see him. When they occurred, we fought constantly. It was time to get rid of him, and I saw no way to accomplish this. My mother seemed to have forgotten her promise.

Once he came home during the day. Finding me alone, he said, "Come on, let me kiss you, little miss sulky. I told you your mother wouldn't believe you. You were very wrong, but if you want, there is still time."

"Wait," I said, "someone's coming up. I think it's my mother. I want to answer you in front of her. My dear mother," I said when she entered, "come give me advice. This gentleman proposed to me just now. What do you think I should do?"

He looked at me, shrugged, and said to my mother, "Truly, your daughter is insane. She makes things up to make you and I quarrel."

My mother did not respond.

"Don't you remember what I told you?" I said to her. "Were you mocking me when you promised that you were going to leave him? Did you think, without that promise, that I would stay here? Go on, say something!"

My mother lost her temper with me, telling me that she couldn't trust me, that she was tired of this, that anyone who wanted to leave was free to go.

Her words fell on my heart so heavily that it stopped beating.

I began to cry and said, "He didn't miss you more than he chased after me. You'll regret this." I hurled myself toward the door.

Vincent stepped in front of me to keep me from leaving. He asked my forgiveness for causing all of this. He begged me to stay, saying that if he had to, he would leave at once.

What could I do? I didn't know anyone. I didn't have a single relative in Paris. The only place I had worked was closed off to me. I had only had one affection: my mother! Only one support: my mother! This support and this affection were gone. I was alone.

I went back to my room. I saw him embrace my mother on the other side of the glass-paned doors. My heart rose in my throat.

If I could escape! If I were sixteen! A terrifying idea crossed my mind. I chased it away, but it came back stronger. I fell asleep counting my age to the day.

I dreamed of Denise, of the advice and suggestions that she had given to me. I dreamed I took a carriage, that I gave the driver an address that he remembered—unluckily for me, it was that deep in my memory—and I returned to my burning bed in those houses of nightmare and anxiety. I believed myself avenged.

I awoke under the influence of these catastrophic visions, armed with a somber bravery. The evil demon had grabbed hold of me. He would not release his prey.

❧

I counted the days, the hours. At every encounter, in every argument, I said, "Good! Good! In two months, in two weeks, I'm leaving you and never coming back. I will be rich; I won't need you." The sweet moments of my life—up to then so innocent and simple—were erased from my memory. I opened my imagination to bizarre, impossible situations.

Having only seen the most limited, the most miserable side of life, I aspired to throw myself toward the farthest horizon, which I populated with phantoms based on what I'd seen at theaters. I was out of my mind!

The state of my soul may have been incomprehensible for Maman and Vincent, the fierceness of my resolution may have been unbelievable. They were happy to get rid of me one way or another. They couldn't fight my appeal to move out. Life became unbearable for everyone. I was so horrified by the weakness of my mother I couldn't even look at her.

A terrible thought came to me. Before leaving altogether, I would make one last stand.

"Look," I said, "I want to convince you. Pretend you're going to spend the day out of the house. Hide in my room, listen, and you'll see if I'm lying."

She hesitated but eventually agreed. We decided to do it the next day.

Vincent came in at nine o'clock. "Where is your mother?" he asked.

"She hasn't come home."

He paced around the room without saying a word, then he picked up a book.

I anxiously watched from near my room, thinking that my mother would triumph if this experiment turned against me. Then my hate rose above all other feelings. I approached him.

"You were right when you told me she wouldn't believe me. You have to leave her to her fate. If I loved you as much as she loves you, what would happen?"

He looked at me without answering. He seemed to see my curtain move.

I stepped closer to him. "You don't talk to me anymore. You can see that I was right not to accept. If I had left with you, you wouldn't love me anymore."

"Try," he said, and he gave me a look that forced me to lower my eyes.

"Try what?"

"To come with me, be my mistress."

"Fine! And Maman?"

"She's weak and fickle. She'll console herself."

We heard a noise in my room. He looked at me. I smiled without a word.

He ran to open the door. My mother fell across the threshold. He carried her to her bed. She was unconscious.

Then he had real regret. He held her; he asked her forgiveness. "I'm a bastard! Poor woman, I killed her! My God, forgive me! Jeanne, my love, come back. I don't deserve your affection. Find me: everything I am worth is here."

My mother opened her eyes, looked around her, and dissolved into tears. I didn't dare go near.

"Leave," she said to us. "Both of you go. I want to be alone."

Only Vincent obeyed this order.

"Where do you want me to go?" I asked, and I sat down.

She hid her face and said no more.

My heart jumped for joy. I had taken back my rightful place in the house. Once Vincent was cleared out, I was quite certain of earning back a little of the time that I had lost in my mother's heart.

But if I knew my mother, I still didn't know Vincent. Not only did he not leave, but he didn't even pretend to.

There are beings that cannot be defended; he was one of them. If you didn't know this man was an untamed womanizer, he would be the best and sweetest man you've ever met. He performed a masterpiece of resignation and patience. He used all of his obedient, easy, and caring qualities to pull himself from the depths where his vices had made him fall.

My mother kept to her bed for a week, with periods of fever, delirium, and exhaustion. He nursed her the entire time with passionate tenderness. In order to get him out of this bed, he wanted to force me to make a scene, spark a scandal. It was audacious, because he didn't want to scare me off completely. But in the state my mother was in, such a scene would kill her. He sensed that I lacked that kind of conviction, and he took advantage of it.

My mother told him to go; she reproached him bitterly. It all slid off him. No one was ever less bothered. He begged my mother to forgive him, and he got down on his knees in front of her. He made the most beautiful vows in the world for their future and said his mistakes were due to the fog of drink, an instant of idiocy. He asked me to speak on his behalf.

I received him as he deserved. But I saw with terror that he'd won the battle, and yet again he'd achieved his goal.

My mother softened…toward him. The look in her eye changed. She must have been through a lot. I wanted him to suffer for her.

Next he asked me for time to arrange his affairs for leaving the house, but he dragged things out, and my mother no longer pressed him to go. All hope was lost. He took her from me.

I counted. I would be sixteen in one month!

They spoke of marrying me to a laborer to get me out of the house. I refused; the man they talked about was not my type. Laborers scared me. I still thought of scenes from the insurrection in Lyon. I didn't have the discernment to see the difference. They said *laborer*, I said *insurgent*. It's a ridiculous error and one that I could not be talked out of for a long time after. I refused to marry, and I don't regret it. I'd done well in not agreeing to marry an honest man who I would eventually deceive or turn bad.

I was made to look rotten. Without having any authority to do so, Vincent was pushing for my departure.

All the affectionate links between my mother and I were broken. A month later, they got rid of me. I was sixteen! And my resolve was steady.

❧

I found myself in an awful situation, and one day I feared for my life. My fate was decided within a few hours with a punch of despair. This was the worst day of my life. That morning, I was innocent; that evening, I was ruined. Many women have fallen into this abyss, but I'm proud to think that no one sounded these depths better or faster than me.

On this particular day, I realized that I was dead—at least, dead in the sense of being able to return to the world I'd lived in up to that point. I would give half my life to atone for the things I've done, but there are ladders that I can no longer climb back up. I accepted my damned status and said goodbye to happiness. If this is a narrative of one's fall from grace, then I would say that here is its inciting incident. I no longer negotiated with the court of public opinion because public opinion doesn't generally negotiate with women who fall where I fell.

That's not to say that I'm not proud of my fellow damned men and women. If I said that, I would definitely hear about it from them. But I was and still am humbled by the sacred virtues of character that I wasn't strong enough to practice.

Even though I never got even an elementary education, I always loved the act of thinking. I kept a journal of my thoughts. Whenever emotions, or challenges, or kindnesses arose, I let a trace of what I'd experienced fall onto a piece of paper, leaving the fragments out of order and destroying them almost as often as they were created. But never did I dream that a life like mine could be of any interest at all—until recently.

Two things that I wasn't aware of were in fact good for my heart. First, I could be pleasant and, moreover, charming. You could chat with me without noticing what I looked like. I'd always thought that the beauty of a courtesan was everything, that no one bothered to pay attention to her mind. The second thing—an equally important revelation—was that my fate, which really seemed so uninteresting on its own, gave me a small advantage in the face of the overwhelming events that started coming at me one after another. It's what gave me the courage to write the story of my life.

But, reaching this point in the story of my life, I see that there are awful memories to relate as well as difficult confessions to make. I would rather not write this chapter of my life and would avoid this confession. I don't know how far this book will travel, but if I have even a single reader, I don't want them to be able to accuse me of leaving out a single shameful episode.

The sentiment that guides me in telling this tale is more noble than the motives that inspired my behavior. I never liked obscene books. I did bad things while admiring the good. I lived in vice while adoring virtue. And I am going to try to recount, as chastely as possible, the least chaste life in the world.

❧

I left my mother's house promising myself I would not return if I met Denise at the brothel where I was going to look for her.

The smallest details of this departure come to mind as if it were happening now. As I descended the stairs, I touched my pocket to make sure my fortune—five francs—was still there. A light rain was falling. I was in my finest clothes, and to protect my hat, I took a little carriage. I gave the address to the driver, exactly as I had in my dream. He was stunned when he heard the street name and number and stood there with the carriage door open.

"Do you know where that is?" I asked worriedly.

"Oui, oui," he answered, laughing. He climbed onto his seat.

The trip seemed long. We pulled up before a beautiful house. The coachman helped me down. I hesitated to go in.

"Isn't that where you're going?" he asked.

"I think it is," I said, ashamed. "If you would wait five minutes, I would appreciate it."

He nodded and sat on the running board.

Having passed through the carriage entrance, I found a gate. I opened it, and a bell rang out. It startled me.

At the end of the corridor was an enormous kitchen. I started to leave, because I thought I must be mistaken. Denise couldn't be staying in such a beautiful house. But just as I opened the door, a voice said, "Who have you come to see?"

I was embarrassed and stammered, "Pardon, madame, I think I'm mistaken…I'm looking for Mlle Denise. Do you know if she's staying here?"

"I don't know anything; I don't know the women. I never go upstairs. I'm the cook." Then she called down the corridor. "Fanny! Wait," she said to me, "the maid is coming down."

I'm far enough from this time in my life that you'll forgive me a confession that is pertinent to the sad tale that the truth forces me to tell: I was pretty. And in the den of sin where I had set foot, beauty was the most dangerous passport.

Mlle Fanny appeared. She seemed very disagreeable, yet after looking me over, she spoke in the sweetest, most soothing tone. "Who are you looking for, my girl?" she said as she came closer to better see me.

"I'm looking for Mlle Denise."

"I don't know that name. The person you've asked after is probably using another. Wait there a moment," she said, showing me toward the bench at the bottom of the stairs. "I'll have you speak with Madame."

I sat down. Almost immediately, I heard them talking about me on the stair landing.

"Is she pretty?"

"More than pretty."

"Bring her up."

Mlle Fanny came looking for me then led into a pretty little room that seemed magnificent to me. A tall, fat woman came in at the same time through another door. She must have been remarkably beautiful once. Her hair was gray; her filigreed headband was decorated with diamonds and rubies. Her hands sparkled with expensive rings. She leaned on each piece of furniture, as her stout size prevented her from walking easily. She was covered in silk and lace sewn with such art that it fell beautifully, even on her body. She asked me for the family name of the person I called Denise. I told her.

"Oui, she is here, but what do you want with her?"

"Madame, I would like to see her, to give her a kiss."

"Ah, good. I was concerned that you only came to

take her away. I don't want my boarders being carried off. It's in their interest—I don't like them chasing after men." She rang, and Fanny appeared. "It's fine for mademoiselle to see the girl who boards with us. Tell her that she's been requested, and that she can come down as she is. It's one of her friends."

Then, returning to my side, she examined me in detail. It seemed that the result satisfied her, because she asked if I wanted a room in the house. She told me that it was lacking most things, but that she would gladly let me stay if it was convenient for me. She wanted to know my age and which house I had been in before then.

I answered that I was sixteen and that I had always lived in my mother's house, but I had decided to leave.

"You're not registered, then?" she asked in surprise.

"Non, madame."

"Then you can't stay here. Leave." And she smiled and left the room.

I was so resolute in my fatal determination that I became frustrated.

Just then Denise came in and threw herself into my arms.

"I knew it was you! I could tell. My dear, I am so happy to see you!" And she kissed me a thousand times.

I couldn't say a word, I was so shocked by her outfit. She had on a house dress of pink satin decorated with swan feathers, a skirt covered in embroidery, and a shirt so transparent I could see through to her breasts. Her hair had been curled the day before and fell in disarray around her neck. Her foot, which I'd never noticed, seemed charming in its gold-embroidered slipper.

"You are surprised by my opulence," she said. "Stay with me, and you can have this too. I'm happy as a queen."

"That's not exactly what was bothering me," I said to Denise, whose naïve flirtatiousness and vanity seemed ridiculous to me. "I'm so unhappy at my house that I would definitely stay here with you. But it seems I'm not pretty enough. The lady who was here said that I should leave immediately."

"Don't be silly, my dear child! You didn't catch that she was joking! Madame is not so stupid as to let you go. When she left you, she came to tell me that you really should want to stay. You're going to be hidden in my room until it's okay for you to go downstairs."

Denise had a point, and unfortunately for me, my fear of rejection was unfounded. As difficult as it is for a young girl in the position I was in to create an honorable life through work, it is equally easy to slide down the slope to dishonor. The elevated minds, the generous hearts that protest against the treatment of Black slaves in the name of humanity should take up the treatment of white slaves. In setting foot on the threshold of this tragic house, I would fall in with far too many passionate conspirators because of this moment of insanity.

Denise left the room and came back after a few seconds. She led me up four floors and into a simply furnished room with two beds. There were two women in the middle of the room playing cards. Another was reading in an armchair. Denise formally introduced me.

"Mesdames," she said, "this is my friend from prison. I've told you about her. She's coming to live with us."

I got a glacial appraisal. They looked me over from head to toe. These women were low enough in the pecking order to require reassurance. You could see that, united by misery and shame, they had an affection for each other that they could no longer get from their family nor from anyone else. There was none to be had. In these sanctuaries of moral suicide, you find all the same obsessions—maybe more so because they have grown in solitude and idleness.

My new companions began to whisper. I didn't hear what they said at first, but I wasn't bothered when I figured out that they were critiquing me. They seemed quite beautiful, especially the one named L. The one across from her wasn't as pretty, but her hands were masterpieces of nature.

Denise left me after a few seconds to return to her conversation with the mistress of the house. In her pushy enthusiasm for the odious life that she had adopted and that she was working to initiate me into, she kept trying to lift the barriers that still blocked my admission to the house. It seemed the difficulties were great—greater than I could have imagined before reaching the depths of the abyss myself.

At this point, I've given a good enough account of my character and personality (and I will for the rest of this tale) to be able to say what's right and wrong. I won't excuse my actions, but I will share them.

When I question, after a dozen years, the memory attached to this move I made, which ruined me and made me pay so dearly, I give this testimony: even the idea of depravity was foreign to my plan. I argue that the most obvious feeling, among the swirl of emotions that agitated me then (besides my jealousy of my mother and hatred of Vincent), was the need to know how to live in this gorgeous world—the world that poor people wished for and dreamed of. I damned myself through pride. My body was more pure than my soul, and that was my downfall. The sacrifice of a young girl's innocence, one who would otherwise be an honest, happy woman with the sainted joy of motherhood ahead of her, only brought up awful memories.

Denise was triumphant. No obstacles could stand in the way of our reunion any longer. I was the most unfortunate creature you could imagine.

The two days that I spent hidden in the house were two days of terrifying torture. The fever of enthusiasm that had come over me suddenly subsided and left me with remorse, discouragement, and great disgust for myself and the life I'd embraced. If I'd still had a little energy along with my despair, I would surely have killed myself. I gave myself a convincing reason to do so much later, but for now my resilience was broken.

If I could erase from my existence one awful moment, I would erase this pathetic house. But I felt so lost and had fallen so low that I no longer had any self-esteem, which is the height of human sorrow. Morally, I was no more than a dead body. The will of strangers replaced my own, as if they'd built an automaton. I was told to go to the police station to register as a prostitute. This roused me from my fog a little.

In order to register, I was going to find myself face to face with my mother, and I trembled at the thought. Nevertheless, I had a kind of strength in what remained of my conscience: a feeling so deep that, without leaving her where she'd left me, without the jealousy she'd placed in my heart, I would never have run away in such desperation.

I trembled even more at the thought of presenting myself before M. Régnier.

"Let's go," Denise said to me. "Don't shake, okay? If you seem frail, they'll take you back to prison; if you're confident, there won't be any problem. They can't stop you from doing what you want if your mother consents—which she'll do to get rid of you."

Mlle Fanny had a carriage brought around. I had sent word to my mother to be on rue Jerusalem at noon. She was the first person I saw there. I thanked her for coming and told her that my leaving was final, that all objections were useless.

"I know very well that you prefer Vincent to me, that you would only leave him reluctantly, and that even if you left him, I wouldn't be able to protect myself from him anyway. To avoid the whole business, I tossed my white dress into the nettles. Propriety, conscience, grief—I shoved them all down! There was nothing else for me to do. No one in the world loved me anymore, and I was dead to respectable society. Don't cry; it's not your fault. You're weak. You were so unhappy. No one would blame you. Let me follow my destiny. I'm ambitious—I'm going to be rich. I've learned to be disgusted by my class. I could never be the wife of a laborer. What you've endured in misery and deprivation, what I've seen for myself, scared me off. My imagination turned toward this gleaming world, which I like more the more I'm in it, even if it's as a slave rather than as some kind of queen of the laboring class."

Evil has its pride too—pathetic pride. I worked myself up as I spoke, and I felt the fever for this life rise anew in my brain.

"This is insane!" my mother said to me. "Who put this wonderful idea into your mind? You want me to accept this life of misery and infamy for you? Yes, I was wrong, I see that, but everything can be fixed. Give up on your plan. Come with me. I promise I'll break it off with

Vincent."

"No," I said. "It's too late."

She knew me and didn't insist.

I was led into the office I'd been taken to before.

"Wait, it's you!" M. Régnier said to me. "What do you want?"

"I would like to register myself."

"You, registered!" he said as he stood. "And you think I'll allow this? I'm going to send you to prison."

"As you wish, monsieur. As soon as I get out, I'll return so you can register me."

He looked at me from the corners of his eyes and said, "And your mother consents?"

"Oui, monsieur."

"Is she here?"

"Oui, monsieur."

He rang and, without turning to look at him, said to the boy who came, "Take this girl to be measured."

I was registered in the infernal book from which you cannot be erased by anything, not even death.

When I walked out, I was overcome by a cold sweat. My hands were like ice.

Denise, who was waiting for me in the carriage, warmed me up as best she could. "What happened? You're so pale!"

"I don't know," I said, "but it seems I've paid a high price today."

My mother was waiting for me on my way out. "Whore!" she yelled at me through tears. "It's *you* who wanted *him*. May God forgive you!" She left without even shaking my hand.

Suddenly all my feelings for her came flooding back. I wanted to get out and run after her. Denise restrained me.

"What are you thinking? You don't want to go back to your house to find yourself between your mother and Vincent. You'll make her miserable, and yourself too. Let it go!"

Vincent's name always enraged me. My heart died.

We went back to the house. The fat woman was waiting for us. First they had me go into a pretty salon where they commissioned a complete wardrobe for me.

I was not given a minute's grace. The next evening, I came down in a dazzling outfit. I'd been given a velour dress with white beads, silk stockings, satin slippers, and a set of coral jewelry.

Denise seemed edgy. She watched our companions with an air of triumph. Their kindness toward me was not growing in proportion to my improved elegance.

The fat lady seemed very satisfied with her new boarder and presented me to her sister, who was called "Aunt" in the house, because it's a kind of family. She was a tall, thin woman with white hair and black eyes. She put on her glasses to better examine me.

You had to live in this hell as I did to know what society in the middle of the nineteenth century, so proud of being civilized, would allow. It's well known that human creatures can get used to the horrors of a prison. The explanation for this fact is very simple: most of these women are stupid. With what little intelligence they have, they die in this life or they escape it. I had only been here a week, but I only had one thought: get out.

Such distinguished and wealthy people came to this house that, lulled by Denise's stories, I imagined that I was going to suddenly find someone who would help me escape. But this was not as easy as I had believed it would be. Time passed, and this knight in shining armor never came forward. On the contrary, each day the chain that bound me to the place of my torment became heavier.

The women who manage these kinds of houses use the weight of debt to crush their sad little victims and keep them in line. It's not just one of them, these misers in skirts, that works this way, as the shade of a money-lender disguised as a woman. They counted each week, and I quickly owed eleven hundred francs.

I was so distraught that they were afraid I might fall seriously ill, so Madame allowed me to go out with Denise. We went to Chaumière. We were so well turned out that everyone looked at us without knowing who we were.

A lot of young men came up to talk to my friend. One of them seemed to pay me particular attention. Every time I turned toward him, I saw his large, dark, kind eyes fixed on mine. I didn't know if this was because he recognized me for what I was, but he had a charming face.

"Who is this young man?" I asked Denise after they'd gone.

"Adolphe?" she said, turning toward me.

"I don't know if he's called Adolphe, but he's the one who spoke to you last. He's cute; it's a shame he's not taller. That would give him distinction."

"True, but he's a charming boy. He studies medicine. His father was a famous surgeon during the Empire, and having numerous clients, he made a huge fortune. He invested this fortune in business, but he died suddenly. The entrepreneurs went bankrupt. His widow and son found themselves ruined, except for a few thousand francs, which they held onto. Adolphe began his studies, but he had the worst luck. He pricked himself while autopsying a cadaver and almost died. He had his arm in a sling for nine months. You can see that he's still pale. It seems it's very dangerous to cut yourself during an autopsy."

"How do you know all this?"

"He's close friends with a young man I know. Don't go around saying they came to speak with us. Adolphe especially cannot be seen with women in our position."

We had walked around half the garden. More young men came to meet us. M. Adolphe again chatted a bit with Denise and asked our permission to come see us. Denise took me in her arms and laughed too loud. She told him that this was impossible, because I was even busier than she was. But the first time she went to visit his friend, she would bring me along.

When we got back to the house, I hated my servitude even more than before we'd gone out. We were only allowed to go out once a month.

I understand very well all the scorn that men have for these creatures. But I understand even better those who, while contained within the sainted joys of the family, can't be bothered. As for the debauched who spend their lives playing around and running gambling dens, they could be more indulgent of the pitiful companions in their shameful pleasures. This is precisely the opposite of what actually happens. The corrupt are the most insolent, and no honest heart could know what humiliation a prostitute has to accept without dying or taking vengeance for the injuries she receives. I don't have the calling.

My fall could neither change my personality nor extinguish my pride. I continued to be headstrong and fiercely proud. During my stay at this house, I had the occasion to work out my belligerence against a man whose fame, glorious as it was, was enough to make him forget about morals.

It goes without saying that I won't name him, but if some readers recognize him, it wouldn't bother me at all. It's his problem more than mine. I'm not embarrassed to speak of my relations with him because, as you'll see, the story of our relationship is not a cordial exchange of money for services but a rapid succession of violence, arguments, and wrong turns.

The first time I saw him, it was, I think, the day after Denise and I went to Chaumière, and I was in a foul mood. It felt like I had to climb out of my depression.

I was asked for, so I followed Fanny into the small salon. There was a man seated near the fireplace with his back turned. He didn't bother to look at me. His hair was blond; he was thin and of medium height. I moved toward him. His hands were white and slender, and he was tapping his fingers on his knee.

I stood in front of him. He raised his eyes. He was a ghost as much as a man, one who'd met his ruin far too early. He seemed to be no older than thirty, despite the wrinkles that furrowed his face.

"Where did you come from?" he said, as if he'd woken from a dream. "I don't know you."

I didn't answer. He began to swear.

"Will you answer when I pay you the honor of speaking to you?"

I blushed and said, "Am I to ask you who you are and where you come from? Do I need to present a receipt? Because I don't have one."

He kept looking at me in a daze.

I drifted toward the side door.

"Stay," he said. "I order you."

I didn't hear anything more, and I left.

I ran to tell the fat woman what had happened. She shrugged and told me I was mistaken, that this gentleman was her best friend and she wished for him to be treated well. He sometimes spent a week at her place, and he was one of the greatest writers of the century.

"That man?" I said, astonished.

"That man."

"Then I'll tell him to write worse and speak better."

Denise was there. She leaned toward my ear and said quietly, "She's infatuated with him because he has a lot of money, but he's an awful man—brutal, dishonest, and always drunk. I pity anyone who has the bad luck to deal with him."

A loud clang of the bell shook the house. It was my enemy, who was annoyed that I'd left him alone.

"Don't go back in there," Denise said.

"Au contraire," I said, looking sarcastically at the fat woman, "I'm not intimidated by such a great genius. There's always a way to be in the company of men of the mind."

I reentered the small salon.

"You're back," he said. "In this house, everyone obeys me. You'll learn like the others."

"Maybe."

"There is no maybe. To start, I want you to drink with me." He rang, and Fanny came running. "Drinks!" he said.

She went out and came back with three bottles and two glasses.

"Let's see, what would you like? Do you want rum, brandy, or absinthe?"

"Thank you, but I only like watered-down wine, and at the moment, I'm not thirsty."

"What does that have to do with me? I want you to drink."

"No," I said resolutely.

He swore like a soldier and, having already refilled his glass of absinthe, swallowed it in one gulp.

"You, now, drink, or I'll make you." He filled two glasses and unsteadily handed me one.

I watched him come toward me, a little unnerved by his threat but determined not to give in. I calmly took the glass that he held out to me, then threw its contents into the fireplace.

"Oh!" he said, taking me by the hand and turning me toward him without hurting me. "You are disobedient— even better. I like that just as much." He put some coins in one of his hands and a full glass in the other. "Drink," he said again, "and I'll give them to you."

"I don't drink."

"Oh," he said, laughing and doubling over, "how wonderful you are! As unaffected by fear as by curiosity. I'm happy either way. Come sit with me on the sofa and tell me your story."

I sat without saying a word.

"You were, is it not true, unhappy and tyrannized? I bet, like your companions, you are at least the daughter of a general. To be blunt, do you like me?"

"Not at all."

"You're not like the others. They're all crazy for me, or at least they say they are. But I'm not here for friendship. I don't want to put up with them, whereas you—you are an original. I like you. Take these coins. You didn't have to earn it; I'm giving them to you as a gift. Leave! Go away!"

I hustled to take advantage of his permission. As I was leaving, I saw that he'd turned to a glass of brandy.

Denise was waiting for me at the door. "I'm scared for you. When anyone contradicts him, he hits them. I came to help carry you out."

I thanked her with a smile. I didn't cling very tightly to life. If he had hit me to get off on torturing me, on humiliating me, he would have been in more danger than me.

I was so depressed that he couldn't do anything to make my life worse. He came to see me two or three times a day. He had moments of madness where he said vile things to me for no reason. It was exasperating. I declared that I no longer wanted to come down to see him, and I was forcefully reminded that my will was not my own. I began to be appalled by the fat woman.

One day I came downstairs with my head held high. Without waiting for him to address me, I said, "What more do you want from me? Why do you keep asking for me? The sight of you disgusts me. If, during your night-long orgies, you do the kinds of things that I read about in the morning, I pity you, because the next day you're not even recognizable as *the author*, and that's pathetic. It makes you feel good to treat women like shit and accuse them of doing what you yourself do. You're not even a libertine; you're just a drunk. If one woman fucked you over, that's not a reason to hate all the others. You might have some reason to yell at me, but then you need to calm down."

I was a little unnerved at the effect of this spirited sermon. He had started off listening with a bemused look in his eyes. But by the time I had finished, he had fallen asleep in his easy chair. I left on tiptoe.

He seemed not to hold a grudge against me, because the next day he came to ask permission to take me out to dinner. Madame hastened to say yes without asking me.

I tried to tell myself that he kept his worst eccentricities within the house and that he was more respectable outside it. He came to fetch me at six o'clock and drove me to Rocher de Cancale.

I dressed very simply, in a dress and hat I was wearing for the first time. My outfit made me happy, or I felt a little less sad anyway, maybe because I was getting out of that awful house for a second time.

At first, I didn't have to do much to make him happy, just listen to his tasteless jokes, or at least not very generous jokes, which I cut off anyway.

The waiter who served us brought a bottle of seltzer water. This gave me a thousand crazy ideas, which had all already passed through the head of this odd man who had chosen me as the target of his whims. He took the bottle of seltzer water as if he wanted to pour himself a drink and instead aimed the nozzle at me and drenched me from head to toe with it.

There are conditions of age and mind where this would be accepted as a prank, but I was upset. His pretending to be crazy was maddening. I fell into a flood of tears—tears of rage. The more I cried, the more he laughed. If I had stayed in our booth one more minute, I would have smashed his head in, even knowing what a risk that would be for me. Luckily I made it to the door of the restaurant and fled, promising to kill myself rather than continue in this line of work for long.

I went to tell Denise what had happened. Luckily she had given up on her absurd optimism, because if she hadn't, I would have succumbed to madness. Denise was far from being delicate, but she was loving. She had a spirited soul, and our circumstances began to weigh on her more than they did on me.

"Be patient," she said, "and please, forgive me. It's my fault. I was lied to just as I lied to you. I see clearly now— all you get is a bad reputation and nothing to show for it. Nothing could redeem anything like this. I'm miserable too; I'm in the powerful rush of my first love. I love a man who would send me away if he knew what had happened to me, and I feel like I could die." She wept. It was my turn to console her and say, "Patience!"

What a life we led, dear God! What torture to have to laugh when you wanted to cry, stay up when you wanted to sleep, be imprisoned when you dreamed of being free. You're dependent and humiliated, and pay so much for the little you possess. If the pathetic creatures who I'm shining a light on here are strangled by the men they're with, they've rendered their service, and there wouldn't be a single one who wouldn't bless the hand that delivered her death.

Love exacts a cruel revenge on women who desecrate its image. Their heart becomes closed off forever to kindness, and it gets tired of running after a goodness that they must always let go. They're depressed because they can't share any affection that they might feel. They may see the contagion of public scorn grow between them and the object of their passion. Even when they succeed in finding real love, the shadow of their past sits at the head of their bed.

The love that they inspire in men is as complicated as their existence. If they can give a man pleasure, they can no longer give him happiness. For these women, to get back on the right track is difficult, if not impossible. If they bluntly say they've been courtesans, all doors shut in their faces.

What about the respectable woman, the mother with a family, who would like to hire one of these lost girls as a worker, or as a housemaid? The girl's fall from grace was no accident, so how could someone believe the sincerity of her repentance? The world is not inhumane; it is untrusting. The wife fears for her husband; the mother fears for her son—and for her daughter above all. She pushes away the poor sinner, not always out of disapproval. Truly upstanding women have hearts full of compassion and pity, but also protection for those they love.

Do you try, then, to hide your past? You spend your life trembling in fear. One mistake could put you back on the road to the life you were trying to hide with a curtain of your blood. For the woman who's fallen so low, there is no family anymore. Your parents gave up on you and are trying to forget you. Marriage is not an option. The man who wants to join his future to yours recoils at the idea of asking for your hand at the police station.

Motherhood, the greatest happiness of all for anyone who considers herself a woman, is the worst kind of torture. The first kiss of your child is a torment, his first word a reproach, because you cannot name his father. Is it a boy? You know that when he becomes a man, he'll look down on you. Is it a girl? You don't dare keep her with you. The past, the present, the future prevent you.

Were you able to escape, one way or another, this gaping abyss, this misery? Ten years, twenty years later—as happened to me recently—you will find that you have an enemy. He'll throw your past in your face, he'll destroy in a matter of moments the results of long years of effort, and he'll push you back toward the abyss without wondering if another fall will crush you.

It's not at all in my disposition to have measured emotions. Joy, sadness, affection, resentment, laziness, busyness—I exaggerate them all. My life has been a string of excesses. With such a temperament and so many reasons to be miserable, judge what I have endured when, to please a man and thus earn my daily bread, I had to put up with the presence of awful individuals. You'd have to have both courage and cowardice not to be Henriette de Janin, the heroine of *The Dead Donkey and the Guillotined Woman*.

I feverishly rolled these thoughts and a thousand others around in my brain. I formed the most extravagant plans, and when I recognized their impossibility, I berated myself for my helplessness. Sometimes, bored with beating myself up, I put it all on society. I told myself it was barbaric to authorize a child of sixteen to sign this disgraceful contract. The law, which doesn't allow you to mind your own affairs until age twenty-one, lets a pathetic girl of sixteen sell her body. I damned Saint-Lazare. I thought—I see you smiling at my plans for reform—I thought that there was so much to be done for the poor little girls abandoned by their parents in the corrections houses. These corrections houses should not be in Paris but in the country so the sun can come through the barred windows and the poor little prisoners can see the trees instead of the high, terrible walls that keep out hope. Nature softens the soul instead of hardening it; their thoughts would return little by little to God, and God inspires devotion. To isolate the wicked—isn't that the dream? It seems to me this would be less expensive, because the children could work. Trying to leave the place where you failed can feel like it's a world apart.

I had reached my breaking point, but I had to pay for it dearly. My moral failings ended up affecting my health. I had a stuffy head, episodes of fever, and I could not stay still, sitting or standing. I felt so sick I went to bed. I was told I must go downstairs after the dinner hour. That fat woman gave little parties for the house's regulars. I don't know what I would have given to get some rest. But I got up without objection.

At nine o'clock there were already a lot of people at the party. I sat in a corner, and no one paid attention to me. They chatted, they laughed; champagne bubbled in glasses and veins. The conversations and laughter covered the sound of my teeth chattering. A shiver overcame me, then a cold sweat. I let myself fall over onto the couch where I was sitting.

Someone got me up and took me out. I was carried into another room. I heard murmuring above my head.

"Poor girl! She's so sick! It's a bout of fever."

"Oui," said Fanny, "she's been complaining since morning. But there's no time to be sick here."

❦

I came around little by little. The person who had

accompanied me or carried me was a young man of twenty-eight or thirty. He was of medium height and had an elegant but reserved demeanor. He held my hand and watched me attentively. He had one of those faces you don't forget once you've seen it: dull but searching eyes, long nose, sallow skin, white lips, silent breath. He seemed used up by work or play.

"You are ill, my child," he said. "You must be treated."

"Treated! Where do you want me to go for that?" Driven by fever, by regret, by disgust for myself, I told him everything without stopping for breath. Then I began to weep. He listened without interrupting, without even seeming annoyed.

"How much do you owe the house?" he asked.

I told him. He shrugged.

"Listen," he said, "if you're interested in what I have to offer: I live alone in an enormous apartment because one of my sisters is coming to Paris after giving birth— that is, in two months. Would you like to live in her rooms? You'll be taken care of." And without waiting for my answer, he rang, asked for my belongings and my account, paid the house, walked toward a carriage outside, and told me to follow.

I asked permission to say goodbye to my friend. He refused, saying that he didn't want me to receive visitors. I asked Fanny to say my goodbyes.

We made our way along the route. My companion didn't say a word. The carriage slowed to a stop, and we climbed out. I saw a carriage house, and I read in the gas-light: Place Breda. We had arrived. The apartment was on the first floor; a man who had been sleeping came to let us in.

"Take mademoiselle to the room at the back. See

that she lacks nothing. If I'm not back, call for my doctor."
He turned to me. "Have a good evening," he said as he
walked away. "Sleep well; it's often the best remedy. If
you need something, ring, ask, it's no bother at all. But
ring loudly—my valet sleeps soundly." I hadn't recovered
from my surprise when the door to the hallway closed
behind him.

I followed the valet, who put me in a pretty room
that was freshly decorated. Once I was alone, I wanted
to visit the rooms that let onto mine. I didn't dare. I drew
the bolt and went to bed. During the night I was desper-
ately thirsty, but I didn't dare call.

In the morning, there was a quiet knock. It was the
doctor and valet.

"One moment," I said. I threw on a dress, and they
had to wait. I heard them talking.

"It would be better if he took care of himself. This
wasting illness will take a nasty turn. And you say he
brought her here last night. Where did he find her? This
will only end in theft! If he goes on like this, I'll write
his father."

I opened the door half naked. This conversation was
making me sick. I said that I understood the doctor quite
well.

He left, saying, "She doesn't have anything."

M. L... returned at ten o'clock, paler than he'd been
the day before. "Well, the doctor says you're not sick.
Which is great! It doesn't change our agreement. Take
care of yourself."

He arranged for lunch to be brought to me, asked
me what I was missing from my toilette, and left until
the next day.

I stayed for a week, seeing him for one whole hour

each day. I would have one good day, one bad day. At last I spent two days unable to get out of bed with a headache. I didn't dare ask for the doctor.

When M. L… came into my room, he recoiled on seeing me. "Quick," he said to the maid, "get the doctor. She is bright red. The fever's going to go to her brain."

In truth, my head felt like a volcano about to erupt.

The doctor took two hours to get there. He arrived out of breath from a lunch in town, which he recounted in all its detail before looking at me. M. L…, always calm, pointed to my bed.

"It's true," the doctor said, opening the curtains to see me more clearly. Then he came over to examine me. "Good God!" he cried, becoming ashen. "Why did you call for me so late? She's going to have smallpox. And she has a fever in her brain; she's burning up. One of these illnesses is treated with cold, the other with heat. It will be very difficult to treat her here; therefore, I'm going to give her a prescription."

He left. M. L… and the valet followed him. I remained alone. I threw myself toward the foot of the bed and listened at the door.

The doctor said, "You can see for yourself it's quite advanced. What will people say if she dies here, at your place? And it's a contagious illness."

"Monsieur can serve her if he wants to," said the maid, "but I will not go into her room."

M. L… seemed very upset. "My biggest fear in the world is smallpox. We can't let this poor woman die like a dog, and if I must take care of her myself, I will not abandon her. But couldn't we move her to a sanitarium, doctor? I would gladly pay for fresh air for her."

"No," said the doctor. "Moving her now is impossible. It would kill her. I'm going to insist you send for a nurse." He prescribed some remedies, and I heard him walk away.

I got dressed. I pressed my head between my hands to try to think. My head burned my fingers, and the heat seemed to eat my thoughts. I took my hat from the table, my dress, my shawl. I opened a door and walked through one room, then another, without meeting anyone. Finally I reached the entrance hall and stairway.

At the bottom of the stairs, my strength left me. I leaned my forehead against the banister to refresh myself. Making a superhuman effort, I shook my will-power into the flaming sword it was. I got into a carriage that I found outside, and I said to the driver as I rolled onto the seat, "To Saint-Louis hospital."

9.

SAINT-LOUIS HOSPITAL

I RODE ALONG WITHOUT FEELING any pain—
because I'd passed out. The driver, seeing that I had
fallen unconscious in the back of his carriage, asked
the doorman at the hospital to help me out. They went to
find the doctor on duty, who had me taken to a room and
then gave me all the necessary treatments.

When I came to, he asked me what I was there for. I
looked at myself and understood: this dress and silk coat,
this hat with flowers, surprised him. A woman dressed
like this wouldn't usually find herself at a hospital like
Saint-Louis.

I told him that I had smallpox and that this had
frightened everyone, so I had come to be treated at the
hospital.

He had me turn toward the light coming from the
window. He swept his thumb across my brow and said

sadly, "Yes, it's true, but it's a great risk you've taken." He took me into a room.

An hour later, I was delirious. I went six days without even a spark of sanity. At last the two illnesses, after fighting over my life, separated themselves. The smallpox alone remained. I was blind for seventeen days; I heard sounds of pity at my bedside. The sisters cared for me with maternal tenderness. I thanked them without seeing them.

Their exhortations to be patient and my resignation to the care of these good sisters gave me a little courage. I needed it, because according to the doctors, my case was one of the most serious they'd encountered. I had a mask of pox on my face that sealed my eyes and nostrils. I asked God to forgive me, to call me to him if he found that I had suffered enough.

Then a kind voice said to me, "It's a sin, my daughter, to ask for death. You are so young; you have time to repent!" Then someone passed a feather and oil over my face, which soothed my ailing body and soul. Sainted women whom God made in his image—what charity and selflessness. Faced with illness, with suffering, with death—and without abandoning your patients—you are sentenced to die, like brave soldiers on the front line.

I heard the doctor ask one morning, "How is number 15?" That was me.

The good sister replied, "Better, doctor. I hope that she will open her eyes today or the day after."

I felt a surge of joy!

"Have you been oiling her face adequately?"

"Oui, doctor, I do it myself every half hour."

"Good," he said, touching my cheeks. "If she doesn't scratch, she should have few scars. There are many spots,

176

but they're small."

"That makes sense," said my benefactor as she tucked me in.

Her hand was near my mouth, and I kissed it. I heard my cheek rasp under her fingers as if it were a paper mask.

"That's not wise," she said to me. "If you end up scratching yourself, you'll scar in that spot."

I heard no more. They'd moved on to others.

❧

Three days later, my eyes began to open like a kitten's. I was warned not to try to open them too quickly, but this was too much for me. I tried too hard, and I felt a little tearing. My eyes opened all the way, though things still seemed dim.

I could sense someone approaching, so I looked around. "You're the one who's been taking care of me! You are so kind. I'm so happy to have recovered my sight so I can see you."

"You're a disobedient patient! If this is how you thank me," she said crossly. "I let you…" And she began to move away.

"My sister, don't leave me or I'll cry. Let me be happy with how well you've cared for me."

"Why did you open your eyes? Now you only have one eyelash!"

"That's the least of my problems. Don't snap at me. I so wanted to see you, to thank you."

"It's God you should thank," she said, pointing to the large crucifix hanging in the middle of the room.

"Of course! Convey my acts of grace to him yourself.

Then they will most certainly get to him."

Vanity is a sin. I very much wanted to see myself but didn't dare ask for a mirror. She guessed my thoughts, because she warned my neighbors to not say anything about how I looked. Advice given in vain! Taking advantage of a moment when the good sister had stepped out, I was feeling so good that a young girl lying in the bed across from mine passed me a sewing box with a mirror at the bottom.

I opened it and brought it up to my face. I let out a shriek of horror! I moved it away, then I brought it close again like a wild animal who's seen fire. I let go of the box and fell back on my pillow. The tears came and deflated my heart.

❧

Number 17 was a woman whose knee was cut; she had had no treatment for it. The injury became so serious that her leg had to be amputated. In operations like that, the surgeon is accompanied by students, sometimes six or eight. This day, they came one after the other, walked around the room, visited some of the sick, and looked at each chart at the foot of the bed, most of which had the curtains closed around them. Two of these young men stopped at my bed and read: *Céleste, smallpox, brain fever, entered the…*

"Hold on," said one, "I have to see this patient who's been spared the worst outcome." He opened the curtains at the foot of the bed.

"Oh!" I was stunned. I recognized one of the two young men who spoke as a friend of M. Adolphe, and the other was M. Adolphe himself.

The first came up beside my bed and touched my face. "She's not too scarred. Look at how she was cared for."

"Oui." His companion moved away distractedly, like a man who looks without seeing.

"Is it possible?" I asked, following his eyes.

"Oui," his friend said to me, thinking that I was talking about the smallpox scars that covered my face.

Adolphe started to move away. I held him by his coat and said, "A word, please? How long has it been since you've seen Denise?"

He looked at me in astonishment.

"You don't recognize me! How would you? You've only seen me once, and since then I've become unrecognizable. I was with Denise at Chaumière three months ago. You chatted with her and me."

He looked for word in response, so he knew what I was talking about. Then, understanding this silence would distress me, he made an effort to pull himself together. "Oui, I saw her not long ago. Since you had promised to come to lunch with her, my friend tormented her endlessly. Denise told us you were in the country."

"I asked her to say that. She doesn't know I'm here. I've hidden myself from her until now. But I would like to see her; tell her so. If your friend wants to see me again, he'll regret it. I'll frighten everyone."

"Don't believe that. He would be charmed to find you again."

"No, I beg of you, don't tell him I'm here."

He promised me, telling me that he would take my message to Denise. Then he moved on.

I heard their heels click on the parquet. I realized that they were coming back to my bedside. I was very troubled. Was it to be pain or pleasure? I think that it was pleasure.

M. Adolphe, his head bare, his hair brushed back, took my hand sadly. "Poor girl, if I had known, I would have rushed here long ago. I'm working in the next room. I heard them speaking of you, so I came to see you. But I doubted that who I thought it was could possibly be next door! Because I've happily been thinking of you," he said, holding my hand. Visiting hours were beginning. He left me, saying, "I'll come back."

I passed my hand over my forehead. It all seemed like a dream. I wanted to fix my hair, but it was falling out in clumps. This bothered me more than the illness. My heart was full after this visit. The next day, I received cookies, candy, sugar, everything that could be sent to a patient.

⸙

Thursday, Denise came to see me. She passed my bed twice without recognizing me. This gave me a bad scare. Finally I called to her. She threw her arms around my neck and sobbed so hard that I had to tell her to be quiet. She was so emotional that she'd set the whole room crying.

Collecting herself a little, she asked me what I was going to do when I got out. I could not count on going back to the house.

"If I were forced to go back there," I said, "I'd be sorry I didn't die here. I don't want to rent a room in some house like that. I only fled from M. L…'s place because I was sick. I left all my things with him. I'm going to send you to talk to him. If he'll send my things to me, you can sell them on to make a little money for me, and then I can rent a furnished room."

"But," said Denise, "you can't. It's not allowed. You'll be arrested."

"That's true. Fine! I will ask M. Adolphe to do it for me. He won't say no. I'll tell him that I am too young."

My handwriting was childish, but I had to write to M. L....

Monsieur,

You were so good to me and so generous that I am embarrassed to ask a favor. I am recovering after a long illness. I left your house because I overheard your conversation with the doctor, and it would have been ungrateful of me to expose you to a contagious disease. I left you the few things that I possess; if you could give them to the bearer of this note, I would be doubly obliged to you. I won't come to thank you myself; my looks now would frighten you. Believe me your most grateful

Céleste

Denise came on Sunday. She had all my belongings plus more than one hundred francs to help me move on. This was incredibly generous on his part. I can never think of M. L... without a brief feeling of gratitude. I've run into him since then. He doesn't recognize me, and he's surely forgotten this memory from his youth. Whenever I encounter him, I follow him with my gaze until I lose sight of him. He's the same as always—slow, serious, and sad. With so much intelligence and wealth, he's never figured out, for the sake of his own happiness, how to rid himself of those qualities in his character.

When I had my things and the one hundred francs, which Denise had brought, I felt a childlike joy.

"You see? I told you. I'm going to rent a little hole in the wall. People say I have a nice voice; I'm going to find work in a theater. I'll earn some money, and once I have a regular gig, I could be struck from the register. M. Adolphe will help me. He promised to rent a small room for me."

❧

Three days later, M. Adolphe told me that he had rented two rooms on rue de Buffaut. My recovery was going well, and my discharge was set for a week from then.

Denise came to tell me that M. Adolphe was waiting for me downstairs and would take me to my new apartment, where he promised to come see me.

The rooms he had rented were on the ground floor at the rear. The window looked out on a boarding school for young boys. At recess, there was a clamor that, instead of annoying me, made me happy. I always loved children. I watched the boys from behind my curtains as they gave bread to sparrows as if they were playing with them. They seemed very happy. When they went back inside, my depression returned.

What was going to become of me? I had enough to live on for a month, but after that…I happened to catch sight of my face in the mirror, and I cried. I could no longer go out. I was so red, and the doctors had advised that if I exposed myself to the elements, my scars would last a long time.

M. Adolphe came to see me twice. The time between

the first and second visits seemed like a century. He told me that he'd been promoted to surgeon at the Versailles military hospital. If I wanted to spend a few days there, the air would do me good. I refused because what he was offering was charity. He gave me his address and made me promise to write.

As soon as I could go out without too much risk, I dreamed of putting my plans in motion. I'd decided to do all that I could to get work at a small theater. I did my hair and dressed as best I could. I put on a black veil and went to the Beaumarchais theater. I asked to see the manager. He refused to see me, but I insisted. He made me wait. After almost two hours, he called me in.

He was a fat man and negligent in his grooming. His hair was greasy. I thought that he'd forgotten to comb it that day.

"What do you want?" he said, looking me over from head to toe.

"Monsieur, I want to work in the theater."

"You think this is how it's done? Where are you from?"

I wanted to say, *My house*. This probably wouldn't satisfy him, and it'd be over before it started.

He got up and, pushing me toward the door, said, "You've never acted?"

"Non, monsieur, but I'll try if you let me."

We were at the door. "They're all the same. They figure all they have to do is find a manager and say, 'I'd like to act.'" He scowled.

I never liked to beg. It made me as bad as him. I opened the door, but as I was about to close it behind me, I said, "It seems to me, monsieur, that no one is born acting. When you're a little kid, you use paper dolls. I'm old enough now to want to learn. I thought it made sense to do it in a small theater. I was wrong. I'm going to try at a more important one."

My leaving seemed to irk him, because he said, "L'Opera is on rue Le Pelletier."

"Thank you, monsieur. I'm going to petit Lazary!"

Once I was in the street, I realized that if everyone was like him, I would have to give up my dream. I came to the boulevard du Temple and went in the Délassements. This manager questioned me while smoking a pipe. He sent me away even less politely than the first man.

I went two doors down. A man who looked like an old woman in disguise ushered me into a small side room with Director written on the door.

He sat in his easy chair with his hands in his pockets and chatted with me for an hour. All the while, he rubbed his fat belly and his gray hair.

He grabbed a big pinch of snuff and said, "We're missing a backup dancer. Can you dance in her place tonight?"

I said I was sure that, if someone showed me how, I could learn very quickly.

"Fuck off!" he said while wiping off the tobacco that had dropped onto his tie. "They promised to send me an experienced chorus girl from l'Opera. I listened to you for an hour thinking you were her."

I was sixteen and a half! I left, red with irritation.

I went to Funambules. I went in boldly, deciding to only leave after I'd bothered everyone. Pantomimes were performed there; surely I was good enough for that! Was I ever wrong. You wouldn't have wanted to hire me. I was too thin, and I didn't have strong enough wrists. These women fought on stage with sabers.

I went back to my apartment, my heart deflated, my legs worn out.

❧

The next day, Denise came to see me. She was surprised to see how clear my skin was and told me that I would not be pockmarked. I admit, this made me happy.

"I came to spend the day with you; or rather, I came looking for you. I'm taking you to dinner with one of our old acquaintances."

"Who?"

"Guess."

"You're crazy; how could I guess?"

"Marie la Blonde! You know, the one who wrote to me the Sunday I met you at mass. She just bought some furniture. We're going to welcome her to her house on rue de Provence."

There are two roads in life: the road to heaven and the road to hell, just as there are two kinds of relationships and intimacies. I was on the road to hell. I was destined to create my social circle out of women who walked the same road I did. I accepted Denise's invitation.

Mlle Marie had a little apartment on the ground floor decorated with blue wool and white muslin curtains. This flattered her complexion, and I found her very pretty. She was stretched out on a divan.

"There you are, my friend. I'm very happy to see you both. Are you coming to dine with me?"

"Oui," answered Denise, who was completely at ease. She moved about Marie's place as if it were her own. "I took the liberty of bringing along Céleste."

"Excellent, thank you for bringing her."

"Isn't it nice here?" Denise said to me.

"Oui," said Marie, "but it's my sixth place; they keep being sold out from under me."

"Well, of course. You sign leases and don't pay the rent."

"This time I'll pay them!" She turned to me. "Where do you live?"

"I'm staying on the rue de Buffaut."

"Furnished?"

"Oui, but I get bored there on my own."

"Would you like to come live with me?"

I looked at Denise, who said, "Hold on, that's not a bad idea; you wouldn't have to pay anything. But you two don't have the same personalities at all."

"I'm not awful," said Marie, taking my hand.

"I accept, but on the condition that I pay half the rent as soon as I am able."

"If that's the only way keep you around," said Marie, "I agree."

My month was up at my place. The deal was sealed when I moved in the next day. I couldn't sleep, I was so happy.

I lived with Marie for several months. She was wonderful! But she was not at all tidy, and we moved every three months. She was surprised every day that her furniture hadn't been repossessed. We didn't go out, but this bohemian lifestyle—without being any more respectable than the life I was trying to leave—disgusted me less.

When we went to some dinner or supper or other, I was not the prettiest one there, but I was the most fun and usually the least stupid.

Sometimes I spent a few days at Versailles. My liaison with M. Adolphe was very much the most precious thing

I held in my heart. I have such deep, lasting feelings for him, even now. There is, in a first love, a magic that can never be found again. When I realized that I adored him, I made plenty of space for him in my life. This made me miserable, because he was far from loving me as much as I loved him. But he was very kind and did what he could for me—even more than he could.

I had opened an account at la Casse to save money. I deposited ten francs, twenty francs on Sundays—without missing a single one.

When I had three hundred francs, I went to Marie's furniture vendor. I innocently asked her if she would furnish a room for me for three hundred francs. This turned out to be the greatest scam on the planet.

She responded that she liked me, so she would. She would rent the room in her name, and I would pay fifty francs in rent. These terms wouldn't pass muster in the business world; I would end up paying much more than she paid for the room. For a thousand francs' worth of furniture, I would give her two thousand francs.

I didn't have a choice. I accepted knowing full well what was going on.

Marie was quite upset when she learned I would be moving out.

"You're going to leave me?" she said. "Goodbye budget! In a month I won't have anything."

"I'll come back often. We'll go out together, and you'll dine with me if you want. But you understand, my dear Marie, that I can't live with you forever."

"This is awful. When you're gone, my room is going to seem so sad! I'll not bother to come in here anymore."

"You won't do that, my dear Marie. You're young and pretty, but you won't always be. You spend everything without thinking of the future. You have to set a little money aside."

"As if I could! When I have money, it's like snow. As soon as I close my hand around it, it melts."

"But when you're old, what will you do?"

"I'll never get old," she said, laughing "I'll kill myself while I'm young."

"People say that, but they never do it. You have to be brave, and you have to be able to sleep at night."

She began to laugh in a way so strange that I was convinced that she believed what she said. I felt the same premonition as she did about the future that awaited her.

⁂

Several days after I'd moved into my new room, I received a visit from M. Adolphe. He came to ask me to go with him to a small party being given by one of his friends at Versailles.

I accepted. I put on the best that I had: a dress of black gauze. It was certainly not pretentious. I was very modest but happy to be with him, because I had long suspected that he had another liaison within his circle of friends. At first, nothing happened at the party to confirm my suspicions.

I was asked to sing, and I did my best. I had been endowed with a great reputation for being fun, and I was obliged to uphold it. Everyone complimented me, and M. Adolphe seemed proud of me.

Then all of a sudden the scene changed. A woman entered the salon. She was dressed beautifully, and everyone gave her a little nod, which said she was someone sure of her status.

"Here is Louisa Aumont," cried many of the young men.

Our eyes met, and there was a flash of hatred and jealousy.

Louisa Aumont went right to the owner of the house, cornered him in the hallway, and said loudly enough for everyone to hear, "I asked you not to invite women, especially that one! I told you what she was. I don't want to be in the company of girls like that."

Where did she get that kind of audacity? Was it jealousy making her go wild? Did she really know the secret of my history? All the blood drained from my heart. M. Adolphe pressed his lips together, but he let this insult pass.

I got up. Everyone had heard; no one dared come near me. I approached Adolphe and said in a voice full of fury, "You should have asked Madame for permission to bring me. If you don't dare to defend me, will you at least have the courage to follow me out?"

"Why do you want to leave?" he said, embarrassed. "You're here, stay here."

I understood. My doubt became certainty, and I took off like a shot.

The door hadn't closed behind me when I began to sob. I waited two hours in the street, hoping he was worried about me, thinking he was going to find me. But nothing! I was frightened by my despair. I ran toward the road to Paris, and I walked all night, listening to my footsteps. It sounded as if the wind called to me. I turned, I stopped, and then, doubting my senses, I started walking again.

I arrived at home destroyed by fatigue, and even more destroyed by my emotions. I waited, I hoped, for a letter to come the next day, a word of explanation. Nothing, nothing. Not an apology, not an excuse, no sign that he even remembered.

This first deception was the most regrettable of my life. A kind and genuine affection could have saved me from my state of mind.

I became ambitious and relentless.

Marie saw the change in me, despite the efforts I made to hide my troubles and keep these new feelings that stirred within me to myself.

"What's going on with you?" she constantly asked me. "You seem so sad, so preoccupied."

"It's nothing."

"You're lying. You're hiding something from me."

She insisted with such perseverance that I felt my heart open and I let my secret out. "I love a man who doesn't love me. I love him entirely, purely. He uses me and toys with my heart. I've put up with a lot; my soul has hardened. He will love me one day. I want him, and I will make him feel what I've felt. When I burn through this love, I'll hate the spark that drew me to him. I have a new obsession: to be in the top tier of these lost women they all admire so much! Who they love! Why? Probably because they're wealthier. My heart and soul are dead. I may only be an automaton now, but this automaton will be covered in cashmere, lace, and diamonds. When I was a thousand times prettier, what were my beauty and my youth compared to that? I'm not so ugly that I scare people; I even hope to be better in a year or two. I'll wait. I have a will of iron. I'll become like Louisa Aumont."

"What is Louisa Aumont?"

"Louisa Aumont! She's my rival." And I told her all about the scene at Versailles, the humiliation I had been subjected to, how M. Adolphe had abandoned me.

Marie seemed as put off by my plans for vengeance

as I had been some days before about her thoughts of suicide.

"Instead of grinding on this away all night, like you do, you would maybe be better off going to see your friend and making up with him. Don't be arrogant when you're in love."

"To each his own. I'll never stoop to begging."

"I give you a week."

"You'll see. He loves this woman, but he'll come back. I'll make sure that he hears more and more about me! It's her opulence that makes him happy. I'll have more of it than her."

"Come to the ball at Chaumière tonight," Marie said.

"No, the one at Mabille!"

"Is it nice?"

"I don't know."

"I've never been there. I'd rather go to Chaumière."

"Then I'm not going out. I don't want to run into him. He's coming into Paris, so that's where he'll be. If I meet him with that woman, it'll be too much."

"You're stronger than me," she said. "I'd be drawn like a moth to the flame."

"No, my poor friend, I'm not stronger than you. I've endured more, maybe, because I feel with a passion that eats me alive. The tiniest thing for everyone else hits me hard. When I want to have something, to close the distance between me and it, I would spend ten years, twenty years, of my life. I am ashamed of my ignorance; I'm burning with desire to learn. When I pick up a book, I want to understand it so quickly that I turn red, my eyes cross, and I have to stop. Then I find myself ridiculously angry with myself and my rebellious mind. I smack my forehead. When I try to learn to write and my hand doesn't obey my will, I punch my arms until I leave marks. If I have hope, I can't sleep. I dream, I'm agitated, I see double. I want to master everything! If my heart is in revolt against my will, I will punish it until it gives in. I'll laugh when I should be drowned by my tears. There is one thing that I will not ask for: pity. Is that what makes miserable men happy? Is that what makes me interesting? I have a woeful soul. If I had a cut on my finger, a wound, I'd be glad because maybe someone would comfort me. But the misery that I feel, if I let it be seen, they'd push fresh spears into the wound. I'll be quiet, but I won't put up with it anymore. The thought of my name being inscribed in that infernal book—the thought won't leave me alone. I don't want it there; I want to erase it. How can I make that happen? Who will give me the means? I try to ignore it, but it keeps coming back. And if, after having made all this effort, erasing my name from that book is impossible for me, I will leave behind life altogether, where I'm nothing but a stain."

"You see, you say the same thing as me. If you were miserable, you would kill yourself."

"Oui, but only after trying to live a quiet life in the future and finally forgetting my own past, if I could."

"You'll do it," Marie said thoughtfully. "But for me, I'm definitely going to die a violent death. It doesn't matter, I wasn't made for the life of a courtesan. But I'm here, so I'll stay here—at least until I'm pulled out by a miracle." She paused. "But what absurd ideas we're filling our heads with. We're going to seem like undertakers at the ball!"

"Don't worry. I'll be more sparkling than everyone! If I run into Adolphe's friends, I want them to tell him that I wept radiantly."

www.ingramcontent.com/pod-product-compliance
Lightning Source LLC
Chambersburg PA
CBHW021143090426
42740CB00008B/916